Christine-Léa Frisoni

THE BIG BOOK OF A
MINIATURE HOUSE

*Create and decorate a
house room by room*

Translated by Stephen Haynes
Photographs by Bertrand Runtz

CONTENTS

Miniature houses give infinite scope for creativity. Whatever the style of your dream house, it can be reduced to 1/12, the traditional scale for this decorative art. You can experience life in different worlds without ever having to move house...

Originally intended for the education of young girls, and designed as records of the styles and tastes of the age in which they were created, these houses were handed down from one generation to the next. Today they are appreciated as decorative objects and as collectors' pieces.

Creating a miniature house calls on a wide range of skills: construction, fitting out, electrics, painting, decorating, detailing... This one hobby brings together most of the creative crafts, and guarantees that you will never be bored!

My technical skill as a modelmaker or miniaturist comes purely from my personal experience as an inveterate do-it-yourselfer. My tips and techniques are based on real-life observation – on the methods I use when decorating my own home.

All my inspiration comes from the everyday, from my enthusiasm for the decorative arts of 18th- and 19th-century Europe. Elegant homes; grand French châteaux; books and magazines on interior decoration; furniture and surroundings which are familiar to me, or which I happen across at the numerous flea markets where I prowl around full of curiosity, eyes skinned for anything worth modelling in 1/12 scale; the colours that I see on my walks – faded, washed-out tones, cameos of powdery whites and pinks, frosty greys... each of these things is a source of creative inspiration.

The whole attraction of this 'art' lies in reproducing, as realistically as possible, objects which speak to you – in preserving the memory of a historical period, with its lifestyle and its decor. My houses don't just reflect my own tastes and personal aspirations: they also bear witness to the gentle pleasures of life, both in the French countryside and in the apartments of the Parisian boulevards... The aim is to recreate the charm of yesteryear in the surroundings of the present, just as you might in your own home.

A number of my own creations belong to private collections, or adorn miniature houses around the world. I thank everyone who has had faith in me, encouraged me and helped me to pursue my dream. I dedicate this book to my friends and family, and to all those who think that houses have souls!

Christine-Léa Frisoni

My studio

INTRODUCTION

RESEARCH

To make a realistic miniature house, take inspiration from real life: personal photos, books and magazines on interior decoration, the property pages, your own interiors, etc. If you have a clear idea of the kind of house you want to reproduce, you can look for particulars and constructional details in books, magazines and furniture advertisements until you find the original that comes closest to what you had in mind. If you have no idea what model you wish to follow, these same sources of inspiration will offer you a wide range of possibilities.

The first step is to decide on the style of the house (grand country house, manor house, farmhouse, your own house, etc.), the region (the materials used will differ according to the region you have chosen), the number of rooms, the type of roof (gabled, hipped, mansard; covered with slates, Mediterranean-style tiles, zinc, thatch…). Then you can establish a plan and determine the dimensions.

Safety note
Miniatures are not made to child safety standards, so, even if they are solidly made, they must not be regarded as toys.

MAKING A PLAN

FROM PHOTOS
It's possible to transfer dimensions from a photo into 1/12 scale. For this you will need a head-on view.

1 Measure the height (H) of the front door in the photo. Decide on the height (h) that you want to make your door in 1/12 scale, then divide this height (h) by the height in the photo (H).

2 This gives you a figure that you can use to calculate all the other dimensions. Simply measure each part of the house on the photo, then multiply each measurement by the figure you obtained in step 1.

FROM YOUR IMAGINATION
Since it's important to keep all the parts in proportion, it's best in this case to refer to the dimensions of doors and windows in the place where you live, and then divide these by 12 to obtain the correct dimensions for 1/12 scale. These measurements may later have to be adapted to suit the house style you have chosen, but by following this method you will have a reliable basis to start from.

Once you have chosen your style, you can draw up a plan showing the overall look of the house from the outside. The height will depend on the number of floors, the type of roofing used in different house types and regions, etc. Front and side elevations and perspective views will all help you to refine your design.

Finally, a plan of each floor, like an architect's drawing, will allow you to work out the placement and dimensions of each room of the house.

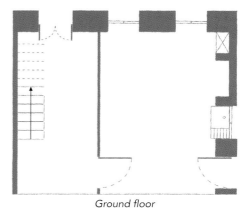
Ground floor

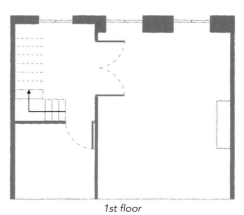
1st floor

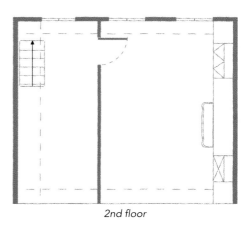
2nd floor

SUPPLIES

The most widely used tools and materials are listed here. These are readily available from DIY stores, craft shops, stationers and retailers who specialize in miniatures. In the following chapters the equipment needed for each project will be listed in full, except for basics such as pencil and ruler.

BASIC TOOLS AND MATERIALS

- Clamps
- Fretsaw
- Jigsaw (not shown)
- Razor saw (fine backsaw) and small mitre box
- Magnifying glass
- Gimlet or lightweight hand-drill
- Hole punch
- Utility knife and scissors
- Pliers (various) and tweezers
- Hammer
- Panel pins or veneer pins
- Glue spreader (not shown; may be an offcut of wood or an old phone or credit card)
- Masking tape
- Brushes, various sizes
- Steel wool, 000 grade
- Glasspaper, fine and medium
- Rags and sponges
- Flat rule marked in millimetres, and pencil
- Florists' wire
- Quick-setting wood glue
- Wallpaper paste
- Solvent-free contact adhesive
- Superglue (cyanoacrylate)
- Filler: this product can be used to create a covering of brickwork or masonry with the aid of a stencil
- Wood filler
- Grouting cement
- Gesso: this matt white primer ensures perfect adhesion of the subsequent coat of paint. Always let it dry completely before painting over it
- Acrylic paint, modelmakers' paint and artists' oil colours
- Quick-drying, odourless wood stain
- Acrylic varnish
- Beeswax
- Odourless white spirit

SHEET TIMBER

- 1. 1mm limewood (basswood)
- 2. 2mm limewood
- 3. 3mm limewood
- 4. 10mm plywood
- 5. 5mm plywood
- 6. 2mm balsa
- 7. 8mm balsa
- 8. 10mm balsa

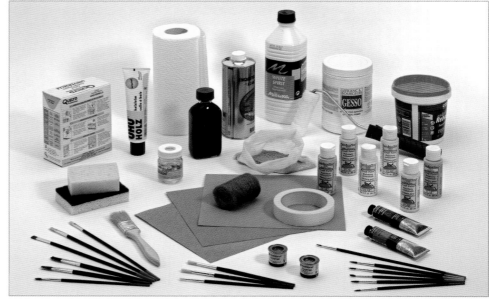

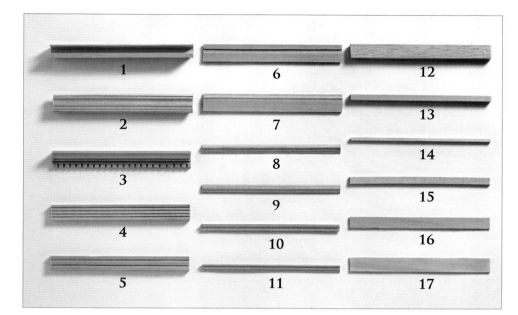

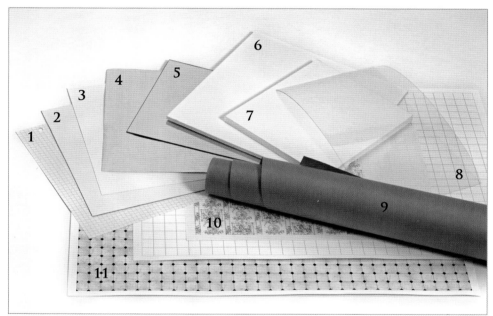

STRIPWOOD

- 1. 9.5mm guttering
- 2. 10mm cornice
- 3. 10mm cornice with dentils
- 4. 3 x 10mm moulding
- 5. 2 x 10mm grooved architrave moulding (or use plain 2 x 10mm strip)
- 6. 2 x 13mm skirting (baseboard) (front)
- 7. 2 x 13mm skirting (back)
- 8. 2 x 6mm asymmetrical moulding
- 9. 2 x 6mm symmetrical moulding
- 10. 2 x 5mm picture-frame moulding
- 11. 2 x 5mm dado rail
- 12. 5 x 10mm limewood (basswood) strip
- 13. 3 x 3mm limewood for battens to reinforce joints
- 14. 2 x 2mm limewood strip
- 15. 2 x 5mm limewood strip
- 16. 1 x 8mm limewood strip
- 17. 1 x 10mm limewood strip

PAPER AND OTHER MATERIALS

- 1. Squared paper
- 2. 1mm Bristol board
- 3. Thin Bristol board
- 4. Imitation zinc paper (thick aluminium packaging foil; see page 188)
- 5. Mirrored acetate
- 6. 5mm foamcore
- 7. 10mm foamcore
- 8. 1mm transparent Plexiglass (and 0.3mm acetate)
- 9. Brown paper
- 10. Wallpaper and furnishing fabric
- 11. Imitation tiles

WALLS AND FLOORS

The sheet timber used for the gable walls and the base is 10mm plywood. Internal partition walls, the floors between the different storeys, as well as the roof and the façade, are made from 5mm ply so that openings for windows, doors and stairs can be cut out more easily.

The thickness of the wall is built with foamcore to save weight, but plywood of the same thickness and dimensions may be used instead.

DOORS

Doors may be built up from separate pieces of limewood, or bought as a ready-made unit, complete with frame, that only needs painting. The latter are available in many styles and can easily be customized.

METALWORK

Metal fittings can be constructed from painted Bristol board or thick aluminium foil. Many different designs in cast brass are available commercially.

WINDOWS AND SHUTTERS

Ready-made windows are suitable for most purposes. They can be fixed or opening, and need only painting. Louvred shutters are also available in different sizes, ready for painting or staining to match the style of your house. The house shown in this book has no external shutters, in keeping with its architectural style, and the windows are made to measure using limewood strips and acetate sheet.

BASIC TECHNIQUES

EXACT MEASUREMENTS

The dimensions of the parts to be cut out are indicated wherever necessary. They are always given in centimetres and in the following order: width (or depth) x length (or height). However, the measurements may have to be varied slightly depending on the material used and the thickness of any coating applied to it, or even on the chosen cutting tool. Moreover, if you want to modify the design shown here, in order to change the decor or the proportions, you will need to know how to adjust the dimensions yourself.

For skirting boards, battens and mouldings, try the cut length in its proper place before gluing, to check that it is the right length. If necessary, you can easily adjust with a utility knife or by sanding. It's better not to glue the pieces until all of them have been cut to the right length. Once the pieces have been glued in place, trim the ends according to the template.

CUTTING A 45° ANGLE WITH A RAZOR SAW AND MITRE BOX

This is the method to use when a moulding has to be cut to fit into a rectangular frame, for example.

1 Use the mitre box to cut one end at 45°.

2 Place the mitred end inside the frame.

3 Mark where the opposite end of the moulding should come, then cut to this mark using the mitre box. Treat the remaining sections in the same way, and all the components will match perfectly.

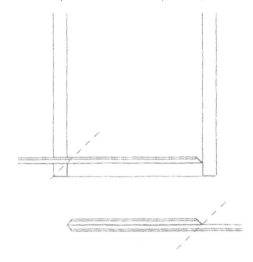

CUTTING AN ANGLE OTHER THAN 45° USING A UTILITY KNIFE AND A FLAT METAL RULE

1 Fit the two lengths of moulding together into the angle, keeping the two pieces perfectly parallel to the two sides of the angle.

2 Mark the points where the two pieces meet on both the inside and the outside of the angle.

3 On the upper piece, score a line between these two points with the knife.

4 Remove the upper piece of moulding, lay it flat and cut along the diagonal that you have marked.

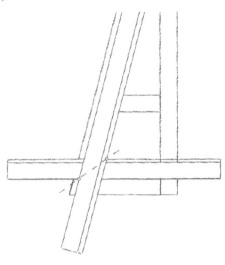

5 Put this cut section back on top of the other piece.

6 Score a new line with the knife on the lower piece of moulding, following the angle of the upper piece. Cut as before.

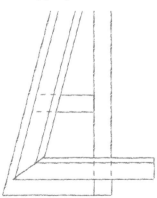

Use this method for all angles other than 45°. It works equally well for right-angled joints (i.e. 45° mitres), if you don't have a mitre box.

CUTTING MOULDINGS AND CORNICES WITH THE RAZOR SAW

For wooden mouldings and cornices, right-angled or mitred cuts can be made more accurately with a small mitre box and a suitable saw. This is usually a razor saw – a fine backsaw designed to run to and fro in the slots of the mitre box without wandering (see 'Basic tools and materials', page 6).

HOW TO USE A HAND FRETSAW

The fretsaw comprises a U-shaped frame, a handle and a blade (see 'Basic tools and materials', page 6). Insert the blade, with its teeth pointing down towards the handle, between the two square washers at the handle end, and firmly tighten the nut so that it grips the blade securely. Squeeze the frame with one hand until you can position the other end of the blade between the washers at the other end of the frame. Tighten the nut firmly. The saw is now ready to use for cuts that begin at the edge of the wood.

MAKING AN OPENING FOR THE FRETSAW

1 To make an internal cut, first draw the required opening in pencil. Now score the outline with a utility knife to provide a more secure guide for the saw blade.

2 At any convenient place, drill a hole just inside the outline, using a small drill and a 2–3mm bit, or a gimlet.

3 Attach the handle end of the fretsaw blade as before. Pass the blade through the drilled hole, then attach the other end of the blade to the fretsaw frame. The blade is now enclosed within the wood and can be guided along the scored outline.

Note
Cutting with the fretsaw is much easier if you start by making an incision with the utility knife along the outline to be cut. This groove guides the blade and improves your chances of following the outline accurately.

CUTTING AN OPENING WITH THE JIGSAW

To cut out a window or door opening in 10mm plywood, as used for outside the walls of a house, you will need a jigsaw. (The walls themselves can be cut to the required dimensions by your DIY supplier.)

1 Draw the opening in pencil. Drill a hole with a 10mm wood drill just inside each corner of the opening.

2 Follow the outline with the saw. The drilled holes allow the blade to turn more easily at the corners. If the cuts are not very neat, don't worry: they will not be visible once the door and window trims are in place inside and out.

CUTTING PLYWOOD WITH A UTILITY KNIFE

Although 5mm plywood is fairly hard, it can be cut with a utility knife.

1 Use the knife blade to score along the cut you wish to make. Turn the board over and score in the same position on the reverse.

2 Begin cutting from one side, following the scored outline. Make several passes until the cut is about 2mm deep. Repeat the operation from the other side. You have now scored almost the whole thickness of the wood.

3 Gently twist the piece that you wish to remove, or flex it up and down until it breaks off.

Tip
When cutting off a narrow strip which does not run the full length of the board, start by making the two short cuts at the ends (across the grain). These 'stop cuts' will prevent the wood from splitting too far.

4 To sand the edges of the opening, wrap a piece of fine glasspaper around the waste piece, which will serve as a sanding block to ensure a flat surface. For narrow surfaces, an emery board works just as well. For a straightforward cut, wrap fine glasspaper around a flat block of wood and sand gently, being careful to keep the block flat and at right angles to the cut surface. It's essential to use a perfectly flat block so as to keep the edge square.

BEFORE YOU DIVE IN...

Making a miniature house gives much more scope for inventiveness than building a full-size house – partly because of the many constraints imposed on the miniaturist by the concern for realism, and partly because each maker invents his or her own methods of carrying out the work.

To make the house described in this book, it's not possible to complete the outside before decorating the interior. For example, the outer covering of the roof cannot be installed until all the rooms have been decorated, so that the electrical installation can be completed. However, you can adapt the methods recommended here so as to create a different style of house, by changing or adding to the decor or by opting for opening windows.

ELECTRICAL WIRING

If you want your house to have electric lighting, you must cut holes in the floors at the construction stage so that all the wires can be brought down below the ground floor. The wires will be plugged into a socket strip located in the basement and connected to a 12-volt transformer. Feed strings through these holes from top to bottom of the house. Use one string for each light fitting that you intend to have, plus two or three spares in case you decide to add more lights at the furnishing stage. This house needs four strings on the left and four on the right; only one is needed for all the light fittings in the salon.

These strings stand in temporarily for the electrical wires so that the latter can be fed through to the basement of the house at a later stage. The strings are essential because of the way the thickness of the walls is built up on the inside: there will be no access to the holes you have made once the walls have been built up. As each room is fitted out, you can then make the holes for the ceiling fittings as and when you need them, and cut a groove in the floor above to house the electrical wire that will be attached to the string. You can cut these grooves in advance if you have planned the positions of the light fittings at the initial design stage.

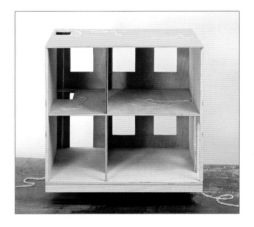

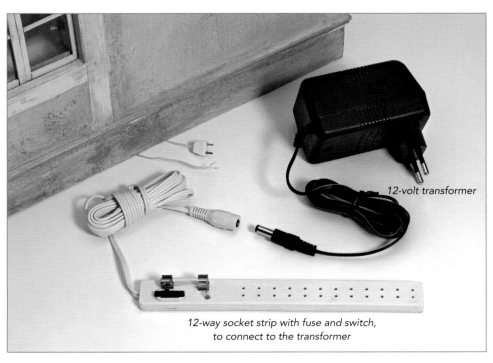

12-volt transformer

12-way socket strip with fuse and switch,
to connect to the transformer

BRINGING THE ELECTRICAL WIRES DOWN TO THE BASEMENT

1 Use masking tape to join the end of the wire to the top end of the string, overlapping them by about 4cm. Fold the end of the wire back so it doesn't catch.

2 Pull on the other end of the string until the wire emerges below the floor and the light fitting is snug against the ceiling.

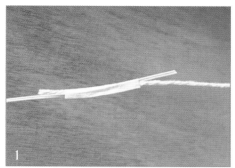

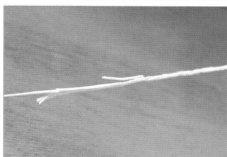

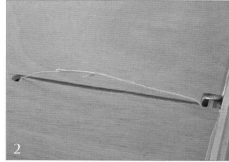

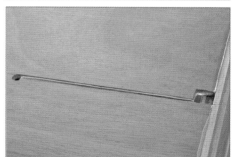

Note
The skirting boards (baseboards) used in this house have a groove at the back to accommodate electrical wires. In this project the groove is not used, but it does come in handy when lighting a house in which all the wires are brought together at the back: in this case the wires must run along the interior walls, and the grooved skirting makes it easy to conceal them.

COVERING THE GROOVES

To allow the wires to remain movable in their grooves (in case you want to change a light fitting, for example), the groove is covered with tape.

1 Note the length and configuration of the groove (straight or right-angled).

2 Cut a piece of masking tape to the same length for a straight groove, or two pieces for an angled groove.

3 On the back of this tape, stick two more pieces of tape along its whole length, so that they overhang the first piece on both sides.

4 Turn the whole thing over and stick it over the groove, pressing down the edges. The first piece of tape has its non-adhesive side down, so the wire can move freely.

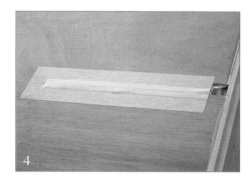

5 To cover a right-angled groove, use the same method, noting the length of each section and mitring the ends. Remember to cut the end of the central piece of tape (the piece that does not adhere) to the opposite angle so it will be the right way round when turned over.

CONSTRUCTION

You will need

GENERAL
- 15mm panel pins
- Hammer
- Fretsaw
- Jigsaw
- Wood saw
- Large mitre box
- Utility knife
- Scissors
- Fine glasspaper
- 000 steel wool
- Squared paper
- Gesso
- Paintbrushes
- Odourless white spirit
- 20mm masking tape
- Quick-setting wood glue
- Superglue (cyanoacrylate)
- Solvent-free contact adhesive
- Clamps
- Pins

WALLS AND FLOORS
- 5mm and 10mm plywood
- 2 metres of 9 x 27mm stripwood

EXTERIOR DECOR
- 1mm Bristol board
- 5 x 10mm stripwood
- Wooden guttering
- Wooden cornice with dentils
- 2 x 5mm dado rail
- Basement moulding (same as dado rail, or plain finishing strip, 5mm wide)
- 2 x 13mm skirting
- Imitation zinc paper (see page 188)
- Modelmakers' paint, white
- Satin-finish acrylic paints:
  - cream
  - tan
  - pink
  - chestnut brown
  - ivory
  - caramel
- Artists' oil colours:
  - raw sienna
  - burnt umber
- Filler

STAIRCASES
- 2mm and 10mm balsa
- Filler

ROOFING
- 5mm plywood
- 1mm Bristol board
- 14 strips of limewood, 1 x 10mm
- Gummed paper
- Satin-finish acrylic paints:
  - grey
  - black
  - silver

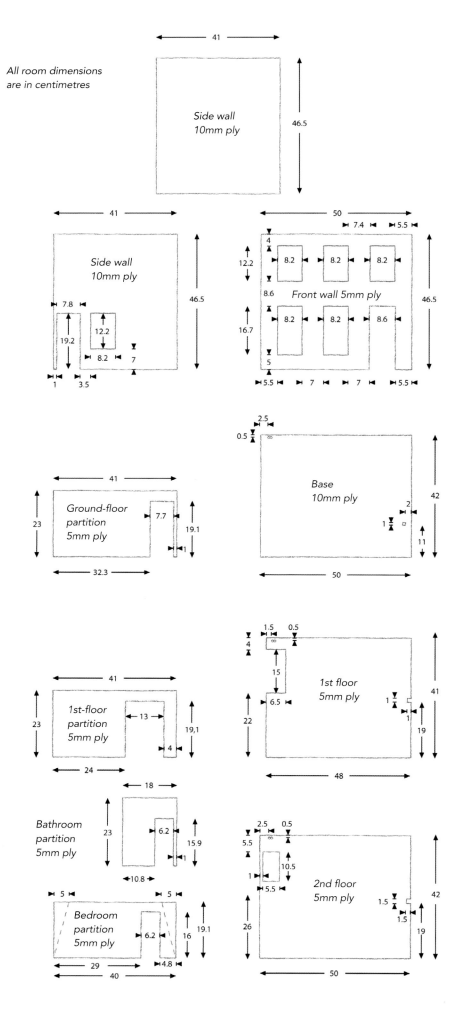

All room dimensions are in centimetres

CUTTING OUT

1 Find a DIY shop that cuts plywood to order. Following the dimensions given opposite, have sheets of ply cut to size for walls, floors and partitions.

2 Cut out the openings for windows and doors in the front wall and then in the side wall. The 5mm ply can be cut with a utility knife or a fretsaw. The openings in the 10mm ply are made with a jigsaw (see page 9). Once you have cut out the door openings, stick the waste pieces back in place for the time being with masking tape, to make the parts more rigid during assembly.

3 Cut out the staircase openings in the first and second floors to suit the dimensions of your staircase. If the banisters are going to be attached to the outside of the steps, the width of the opening is equal to the width of the steps, plus 5mm to allow for the banisters. For the kind of staircase where the banisters rest on top of the steps, the opening is equal to the width of the steps.

Note

To establish the length of the staircase opening, temporarily install the staircase and draw a vertical line from the base of the first step to the ceiling. The length of the opening is equal to the distance between the top end of your pencil line and the point where the top of the staircase meets the ceiling. However, depending on the space available and the requirements of the room layout, the length of the opening may have to be reduced slightly. In our case, the opening on the first floor ought to be about 5cm longer than it is, but this would not leave space for a bathroom on the first floor. For the same reason, the opening on the second floor has been made as small as possible.

4 Cut out the door openings in the partition walls, except for the bathroom wall. For the top floor, cut out the door opening before cutting the angled ends of the wall, to avoid the risk of breaking the wood at its narrowest point. (In order to maximize space along this wall, the door is placed right at the end of the partition.)

OPENINGS FOR ELECTRICAL WIRING

1 The holes where the wires pass through the floors are shown in the diagrams on the opposite page. In the base, drill a hole with a 10mm bit, 11cm from the front edge and 2cm in from the right-hand side. In the upper left-hand corner, make a small opening by drilling two adjacent holes with a 5mm wood bit at the position shown.

2 In the first floor, cut a 1 x 1cm notch with the utility knife, 19cm from the front edge. Drill two holes in the upper left corner as before. Do the same on the second floor, in the positions shown in the drawings.

BASEMENT

1 Cut two 50cm and two 40cm lengths of 5 x 10mm stripwood. In one of the 50cm pieces, cut two notches as shown (these will be the basement windows). In one of the shorter pieces, drill a hole large enough to take the cord of the electrical socket strip.

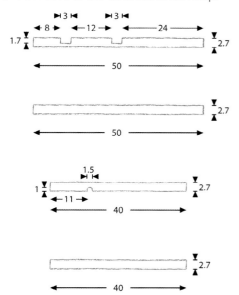

2 Assemble the basement frame as shown, applying glue to the ends of the shorter sections.

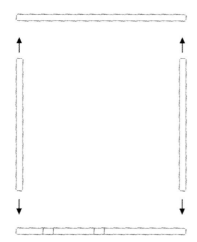

3 Glue the upper edge of the frame and fix the base on top.

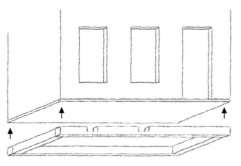

You will need

DORMER WINDOWS
- 10mm balsa
- 2 x 10mm limewood strip
- 1mm Bristol board
- Imitation zinc paper
- Satin-finish acrylic paints:
    English rose
    chestnut brown
    ivory
    caramel
- Filler

CHIMNEY
- 6mm and 10mm balsa
- Filler
- 2 wooden chimney pots
- Satin-finish acrylic paint, cream

FLASHING AND ROOF COVERING
- Imitation zinc paper
- Modelmakers' paint, silver
- Incense paper (papier d'Arménie)

WINDOWS
- 2 x 5mm limewood strip
- 2 x 2 and 5 x 10mm limewood strip
- 0.3mm acetate sheet

WINDOW TRIM
- 2mm dowel
- 1 x 5mm limewood strip
- Thin Bristol board
- Small oval beads
- Modelmakers' paints or satin-finish acrylics:
    off-white
    white
    soft green
    light grey
    tan

DOORS
- Ready-made semiglazed door and frame, 7.6 x 19cm
- 2mm limewood sheet
- 2 x 5 and 2 x 10mm limewood strip
- 2 x 2 and 5 x 10mm strip
- 0.3mm acetate sheet
- Gold-coloured doorknob and bolt
- Satin-finish acrylic paints:
    off-white
    white
    soft green
    light grey
    tan
    straw yellow

HINGES
- 1.5mm florists' wire
- Thick metal foil
- 3mm mini-nails

ASSEMBLING THE HOUSE

1 On the inside face of the front wall, draw a line 19.5cm from the left-hand side to indicate the position of the partition walls. On each floor, draw a corresponding line 18.5cm from the left edge.

2 Glue and pin the sides to the base, so that the base protrudes 5mm front and back. Attach the front wall, which fits into one of these 5mm overlaps. Use masking tape to hold the parts in alignment.

3 Temporarily tape the partitions to the insides of the house walls. These will serve as a guide to keep the first floor square to the walls. Glue and pin the first floor, then the second, butting the edges against the front wall. You now have a five-sided 'box'.

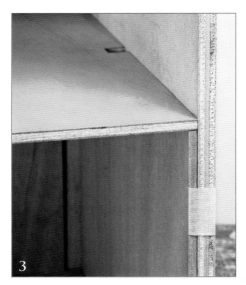

4 Glue the partitions in place, to the left side of the marked line, except for the bathroom partition, which will be installed once the landing is finished.

Note

At the back, the base extends 5mm beyond the walls. This space will be filled by pieces of 5 x 10mm trim, cut to fit and glued along the edges. The top floor will be finished in the same way, matching the edges of the trim to the slope of the roof (see 'Cutting an angle other than 45°', page 8).

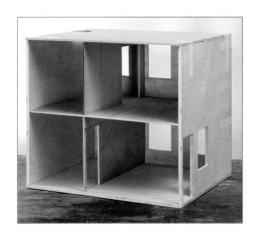

EXTERIOR DECOR

1 Apply masking tape to the parts that will not be coated with filler: a 2cm strip at each end of the front wall and at the front edge of each side wall and 1.5cm around windows and doors. Mask similarly the parts that will have stone facings (dimensions given on page 22), not forgetting the area behind the gutter and cornice just below the roof, the string course (the moulding at first-floor level) and the basement moulding (see pages 21 and 23).

2 Use a glue spreader to apply small amounts of filler to all the outside walls. You can vary the appearance and the degree of finish of this covering to suit yourself (see page 188).

3 When you have achieved the desired effect, gently remove all the tape. The masking procedure allows you to blend the different elements of the decor into the thickness of the roughcast surface, so that stones, bricks or half-timbering all appear to be an integral part of the structure, and not just stuck on top.

4 Wait till the filler is completely dry before applying a coat of gesso to all the surfaces. Allow it to overlap generously onto the parts without filler, but don't let it get excessively thick.

5 Once the gesso is completely dry, apply one or two finishing coats in light tan (a mixture of tan and cream in equal parts), except on the basement area.

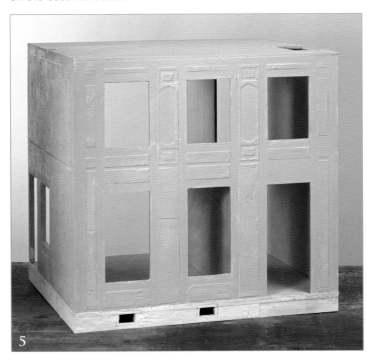

PILASTERS FOR SIDES OF FIRST-FLOOR WINDOWS

1 For each side of each window, cut a strip of 1mm Bristol board, 2.5 x 18.5cm. Score a line 1cm in along the whole length, by running the utility knife along the board without cutting through. Placing this strip upright, make a series of double cuts, less than 1mm wide, at intervals of 1cm, for a distance corresponding to the height of the window opening. Peel off the upper layer of paper from between each double cut, leaving narrow grooves to simulate joints. Cut and trim the bands as shown in the diagram.

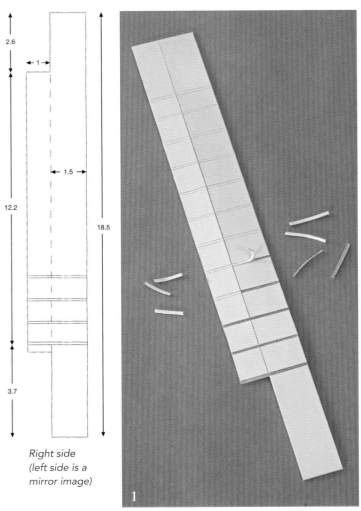

Right side (left side is a mirror image)

2 Paint the strips with gesso, not forgetting the edges of the Bristol board, the scored fold and the grooves. When dry, paint the whole strip cream. When this is quite dry, apply a very thin coat of filler to give a stone effect. Spread it and smooth it thoroughly, but leave some irregularities. Once the filler is dry, bend the strip at right angles along the scored line.

PILASTERS FOR SIDES OF GROUND-FLOOR FRONT WINDOWS

Following the dimensions given in the diagram, proceed as for the first-floor windows. Note the small notch for the window transom.

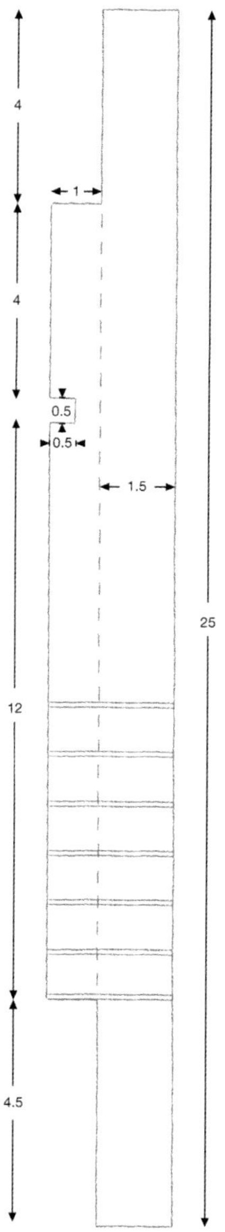

4

1

4

0.5

0.5

1.5

25

12

4.5

*Right side
(left side is a
mirror image)*

EXTERIOR TRIM FOR SIDE WINDOW

Following the dimensions given, proceed as for the other windows, but do not cut grooves.

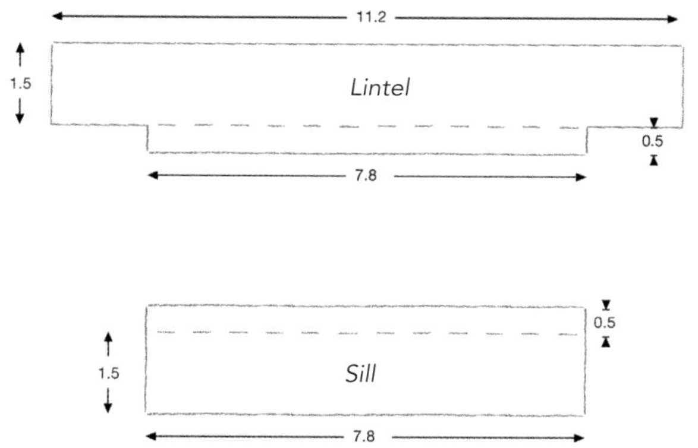

11.2

1.5

Lintel

0.5

7.8

0.5

1.5

Sill

7.8

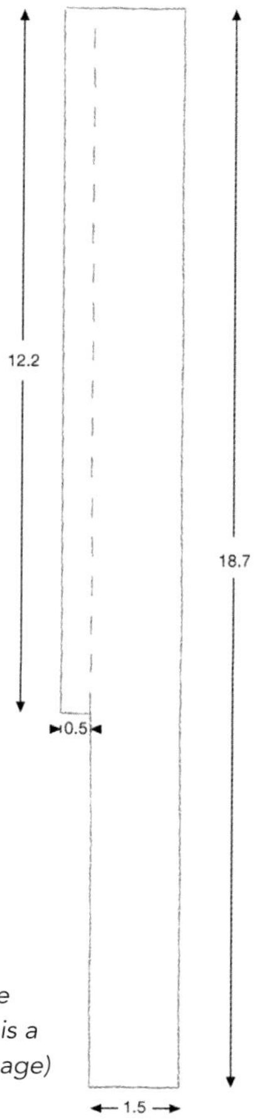

12.2

18.7

*Right side
(left side is a
mirror image)*

0.5

1.5

EXTERIOR TRIM FOR SIDE DOOR

Following the dimensions given, proceed as before, without cutting grooves.

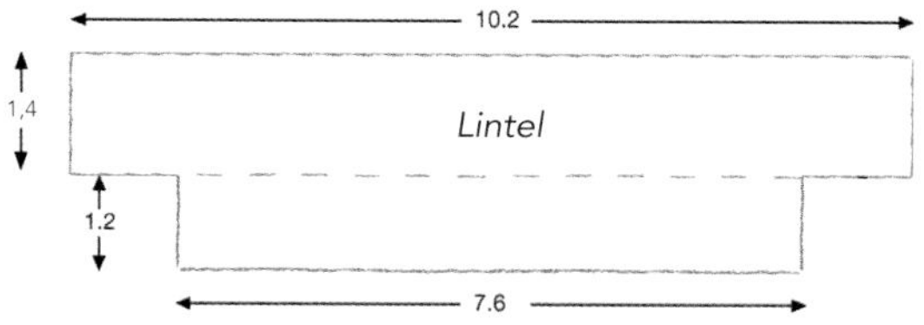

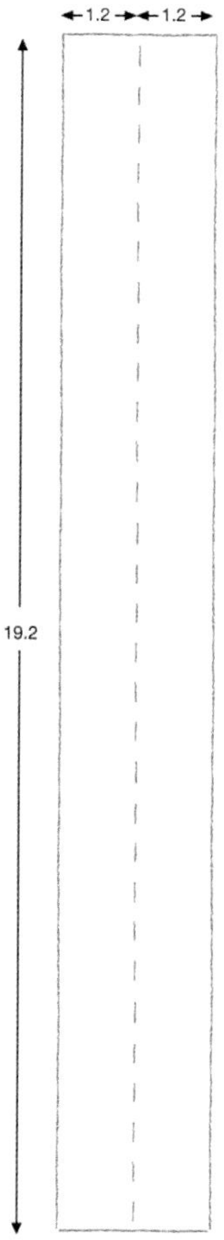

1.2 1.2

10.2

1.4

Lintel

1.2

7.6

19.2

Sides: cut 2

FRONT WINDOWSILLS

For each window, cut a 2.5 x 7.8cm rectangle of 1mm Bristol board. Score 1cm in from the edge for the full length, then apply paint and filler but do not make incisions to represent stones. The sills are left smooth to receive coverings of imitation zinc paper (see page 188).

ZINC COVERING FOR SILLS

For each window, cut a 1.5 x 7.8cm rectangle of 1mm Bristol board. Cover with imitation zinc paper.

FIXING DOOR AND WINDOW SURROUNDS

Start with the sides, then glue the lintels and sills, and finally the zinc covering. Using wood glue, fix the narrower part (1cm) to the inside and the wider part (1.5cm) to the outside, where there is no filler.

Note

Depending on the thickness of the paint and of the thin coat of filler applied to these pieces, it may be necessary to trim the lintel and the sill (using scissors or a utility knife) so that they fit accurately between the two side pieces.

BRICK FACINGS ABOVE WINDOWS

1 For each of the front windows, cut a long strip of 1mm Bristol board, 2.5cm wide. Paint as described on page 188.

2 Using a utility knife and a steel rule, score the whole length of the Bristol board at 0.5cm intervals. Make a second series of score marks at 90° to the first, at intervals of 1.5cm. This produces small rectangles measuring 0.5 x 1.5cm, which are then cut out with scissors following the score marks.

3 Cut a template, 2.5 x 8.1cm, from squared paper. Adjust as necessary so that it fits between the upright pilasters which are already in place.

4 Apply glue evenly to the squared paper. Lay the bricks, staggering the joints so that each brick overlaps those in the previous row by one third of its length.

5 When the template is completely covered, trim off the overhanging ends of the bricks, then retouch the paint on the edges. Score a line with the utility knife 1cm in from one of the long edges, and fold to a right angle. Glue in place above the window.

6 Spread a thin coat of filler over the brickwork to fill in the joints.

KEYSTONES

1 To make the wedge-shaped keystone, cut pieces of 1mm Bristol board to the dimensions shown. Fix the smaller piece on top of the larger with wood glue.

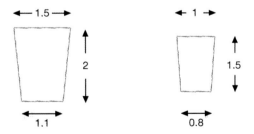

2 Cover with gesso, then paint cream. When dry, apply filler; smooth and wipe off the filler so as not to build up excess thickness.

CORNICE, GUTTER AND STRING COURSE

1 Cut four battens to support the gutters: two pieces 51 cm long, and two of 42 cm. Cut four lengths of guttering to fit, mitring the corners so that they fit all round the base of the roof.

2 The cornice may have dentils (small square blocks) or a decorative moulding. Cut three lengths to fit, mitring the ends to fit the corners of the façade. Cut the dado moulding for the string course (at first-floor level) in the same way. No mouldings are used on the rear wall.

3 Paint the gutters with gesso, then with silver paint. Do the same with the battens, painting only the upper surface which is level with the top floor. Paint the cornice and the string course with gesso, then paint them cream.

4 Using wood glue, fix the battens level with the floor of the top storey. Glue the gutter *onto* the batten. Glue the cornice *below*, on the part of the wall that has no filler. Glue the string course 30 cm up from the lower edge of the basement, where there is no filler.

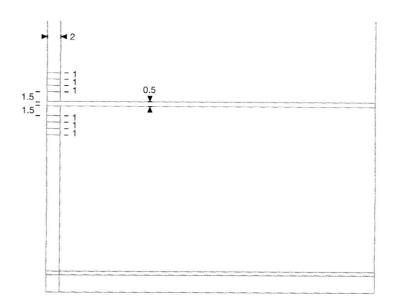

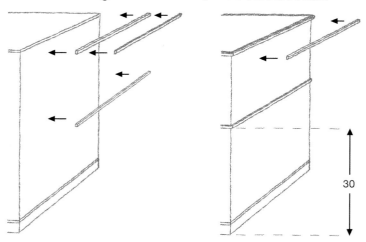

CORNERSTONES

1 For each corner of the façade, cut two strips of 1mm Bristol board, 4cm wide, to fit below the string course and two more to fit above.

2 Using the same method as for the pilasters of the window surrounds, cut grooves at 1cm intervals so as to simulate stones measuring 1 x 2cm, with a larger stone of 1.5 x 2cm at each end.

3 Score these strips along the centreline and fold at 90° so that they cover 2cm of the front wall and 2cm of the side wall.

4 Glue the strips above and below the string course.

FRONT DOOR SURROUND

Cut an 8.3 x 3cm strip of 1mm Bristol board for the lintel and score to represent individual stones. For the side pieces, follow the dimensions given here and use the same method as for the front window surrounds.

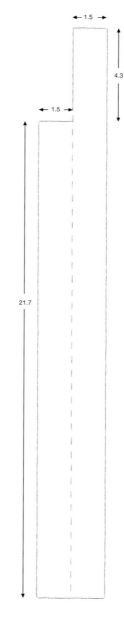

PORCH

1 Cut a 12cm length of the cornice with dentils, and a matching length of 5 x 10mm stripwood. Glue the cornice to the stripwood and glue both to the façade below the string course.

2 From 1mm Bristol board, cut a strip measuring 1.2 x 12cm and five smaller strips 0.3 x 1.2cm. Paint the ends of the smaller pieces silver. Cover the larger strip with imitation zinc paper (see page 188). Glue the smaller strips on top at intervals of 2cm.

3 Cut five strips of zinc paper, 1 x 1.2cm. Place one of these over each of the smaller strips of Bristol board, gluing it both to the small strip and to the larger strip beneath. If the small strips of zinc or Bristol board overhang, trim them and retouch the front edge with silver paint. Glue this assembly to the cornice.

4 Below, on either side of the door surround, glue a 1.5cm length of skirting board upside down (moulded edge downwards).

STONE FACINGS

1 Cut the facings from 1mm Bristol board to the dimensions given below.

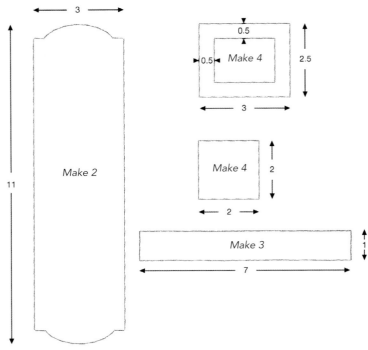

2 Give these an imitation stone finish to match the window surrounds. Fix them with wood glue in the places left for them.

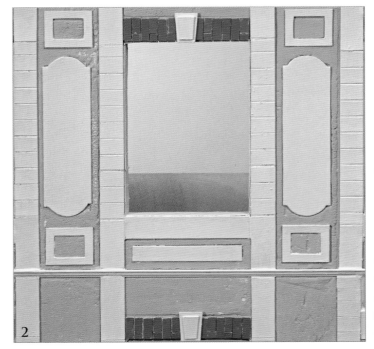

FINISHING THE BASEMENT

1 Mask a 5mm margin around the basement windows and all round the bottom edge of the wall. Coat the basement with filler; before this has dried, remove the masking tape from around the windows only. When completely dry, paint the basement cream.

2 Cut the surrounds for the basement windows from 1mm Bristol board as shown. Make four of each piece.

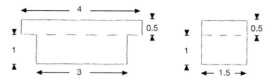

3 Coat with filler and paint to simulate stone, as for the main window surrounds. Attach the four parts of the surround as shown below.

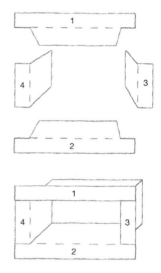

4 Cut three lengths of dado moulding for the basement, as you did for the gutter (except that there is no basement moulding at the back of the house). The moulding stops short at the door surrounds. Paint cream. Glue the moulding in place, 3.5cm up from the bottom edge of the basement wall.

FINISHING THE EXTERIOR WALLS

Once all the facings are in place, apply a little filler to all the edges, then smooth and wipe off with a damp sponge to give the impression that everything is fused together in a single mass. Finish the house with a combination of patinas 1 and 2 (page 188).

FRONT STEPS

1 Cut two pieces of 10mm balsa as shown.

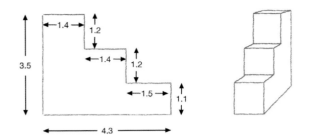

2 Cut the risers of the steps from 2mm balsa: one 1.1 x 12cm (a) and two 1.2 x 12cm (b). Glue in place.

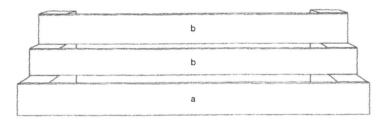

3 Cut the steps from 2mm balsa: 1.5 x 12cm (c), 1.4 x 12cm (d) and 1.6 x 12cm (e). Glue in place.

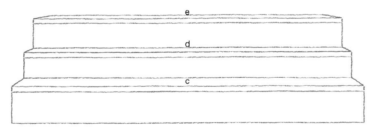

4 Round over the edges of the steps. Paint with gesso. Leave to dry, then apply a thin coat of filler and follow with patina 1 (page 188). Wipe off the patina with 000 steel wool before it dries, to give the required degree of wear. Glue the steps below the front door, and seal with filler where they meet the basement wall.

SIDE STEPS

1 Cut two pieces of 10mm balsa as shown.

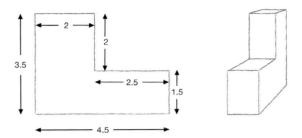

2 Cut the risers from 2mm balsa: 1.5 x 9cm (a) and 2 x 9cm (b). Glue in place.

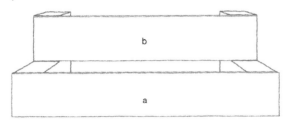

3 Cut the steps from 2mm balsa: 2.5 x 12cm (c) and 2.2 x 12cm (d). Glue in place.

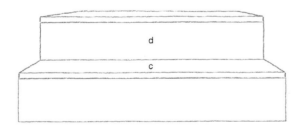

4 Continue as for the front steps.

CUTTING AND ASSEMBLING THE ROOF

1 Cut the front slope of the roof from 5mm plywood as shown. Fretsaw the openings for the dormer windows. Use a utility knife to cut the ends of the roof to the correct angle, starting 6cm in from the top corner and continuing to the bottom corner.

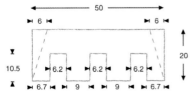

2 On the inside of this piece, at the left-hand end, mark a point 2.5cm in from the bottom corner and another 1cm in from the top corner. Cut a groove between these two points. This groove will face the opening for the staircase in the nursery.

Note

As when cutting out a doorway in a partition with angled ends (page 15, step 4), it is advisable to cut the slanted ends of the roof after cutting the window openings, even though the dormers are not that close to the ends of the wall.

3 Cut two side pieces measuring 41 x 20cm. Angle the ends in the same way as you did for the front.

4 Cut a rectangle 31.5 x 38.5cm from 1mm Bristol board. This forms the ceiling of the attic rooms. It will support the sheets of Bristol board forming the upper part of the roof.

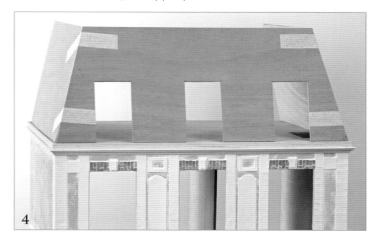

5 Assemble the roof by gluing the front face to the edges of the side pieces. Place this assembly on top of the walls.

SLATES

1 Take a 1 x 10mm strip of limewood, 1m long, and cut it into 2cm lengths, giving 50 slates per strip. You will need at least 13 strips of lime to make the 630 or so slates that will be needed to cover the whole roof.

2 Make a template for the front slope of the roof from two A4 sheets of squared paper. Join the two short ends together with masking tape on the back (the side to which the slates are *not* stuck), taking care to align the printed lines on the two pieces.

Note

Gluing the slates to a template allows them to be cut precisely to fit the roof. This method works just as well on a roof that is already fully assembled. If the roof has not yet been assembled, you can lay it flat and lay the slates directly onto it, but this only works for the front slope of the roof: the slates on the sides have to cover the ends of those on the front. For this reason you will have to make templates which take account of the 5mm overlap caused by the thickness of the plywood.

3 Lay the squared paper over the front slope of the roof, aligning the bottom edge of the paper with the base of the roof. Press with your finger to mark the edges of the roof and the window openings. Cut the sloping ends, then the top edge.

4 Draw round the insides of the window openings in pencil, pressing hard enough to make the pencil lines visible on the front face of the template. Redraw these lines on the front.

5 Spread glue on the lower 2 or 3cm of the template, except where the window openings will be. Lay the first row of slates from left to right, butting them against one another. It's important to lay a full row of slates, even in the window areas where you have not put any glue, to ensure that all the rows match up; follow this rule until the last slate is in place.

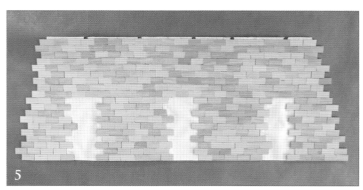

6 Do the same for the remaining rows of slates, always placing them so that the joint between two neighbouring slates is centred on the slate below. As you add more rows, you can reuse the unglued slates from the first few rows. It doesn't matter if the slates overlap the pencil lines: the edges will be trimmed later with a utility knife.

Note

The rows of slates will adhere better to the backing if you fasten them down with masking tape as you go. It's a good idea to leave the work under weights from time to time while the covering is in progress.

7 Once the 19 rows of slates are in place, there is 0.5cm of paper left over at the top; cut this off. Place the roof under weights for half an hour. Turn the roof over so the template is on top, then trim off the surplus ends of the slates with a utility knife, along the sloping ends and in the window openings.

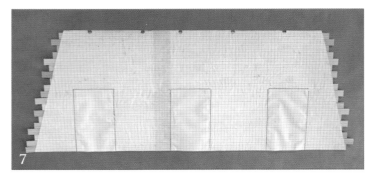

8 Glue the whole assembly to the front slope of the roof. Hold it in place with masking tape, clamps and pins driven into the joints between the slates.

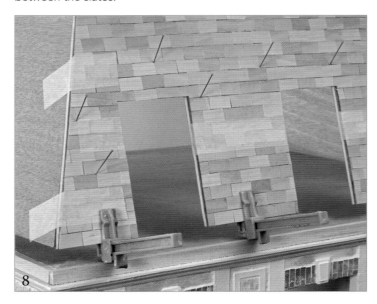

9 Glue on a piece of stripwood to fill the gap left above the last row of slates; trim the edges to match the slope of the roof.

10 Do the same for the two side pieces of the roof, leaving a space for the chimney (as you did for the dormer windows). This is a rectangle 12 x 13.5cm in the centre of the template.

11 Paint the roof as described on page 188.

DORMER WINDOWS

1 For each dormer, cut the following pieces from 10mm balsa and 2 x 10mm limewood strip and glue together.

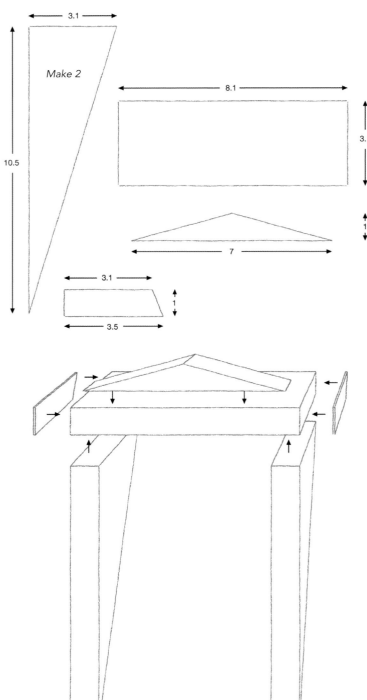

2 Paint all over with gesso. Then apply filler to the sides and gable only (avoiding the front edges of the side pieces) and wipe smooth, retaining a certain unevenness to give the effect of stonework.

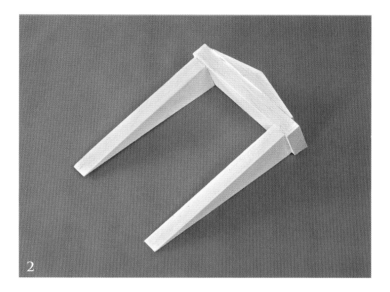

3 The brick surrounds are made as before. For each dormer, cut the following templates: two rectangles of 0.5 x 11.5cm for the sides, and one 0.5 x 6.5cm for the lintel. For the uprights, the bricks are laid horizontally.

4 Glue the bricks in place and glue the dormers to the roof.

5 Using 1mm Bristol board, cut two pieces as shown for each of the keystones. Glue them one on top of the other with wood glue.

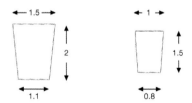

6 Finish these in the same way as the keystones of the other windows, then glue in place. Complete the effect with filler between the bricks and the side walls of the dormers.

ROOFS OF THE DORMER WINDOWS

1 For each of the three dormers, cut a roof piece as shown from 1mm Bristol board. Score down the centre with a utility knife.

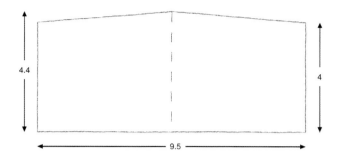

2 Using wood glue, stick the scored side to the reverse of your imitation zinc paper, placing the pointed end on the edge of the zinc paper. Trim the zinc paper, leaving a margin of about 1cm on three sides. Fold over the excess, short sides first.

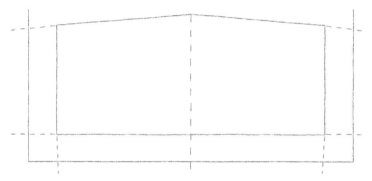

3 Glue the roofs onto the dormers.

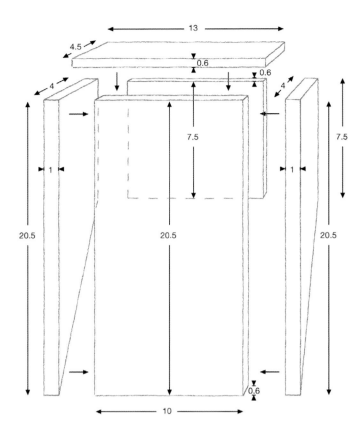

CHIMNEY

1 Cut the front, back and top from 6mm balsa to the dimensions given. Cut the sides from 10mm balsa. Bevel the lower edge to match the slope of the roof; the front and rear faces must be bevelled in their thickness and the sides in their width.

2 Apply filler, then paint and patinate to match the walls. Glue the chimney to the roof and add chimney pots, which are painted terracotta like the bricks.

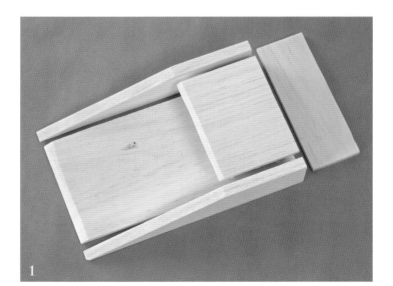

ZINC FLASHING

1 Cut and fold strips of imitation zinc paper to fit around the chimney, as shown.

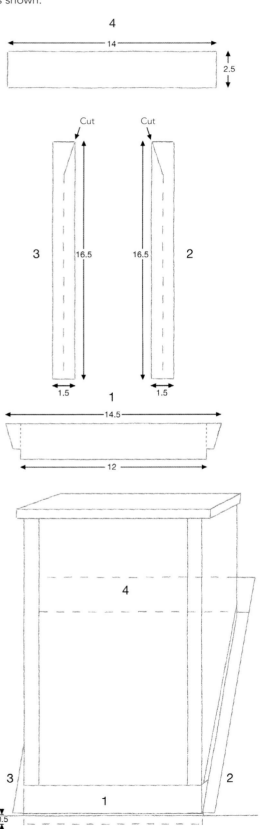

2 Make the flashing for the dormer roofs from strips 1cm wide, folded in half along their length. Trim the length of the strips to fit the junction between the dormer roof and the main roof. Since the dormer roof is made of two slightly sloping surfaces, you will have to snip the zinc strip in the centre to allow it to follow the angle. Cut further strips to length to fit along the side walls of the dormers.

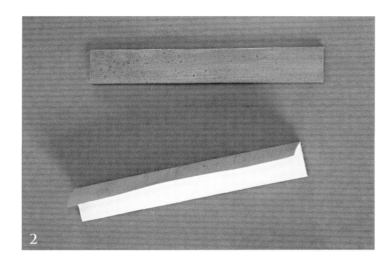

3 For the flashing between the dormer and the gutter, cut a strip measuring 8.5 x 1.5cm, folded along its length 1cm from the edge; mark the fold, then open it out. Lay it flat along the base of the dormer, and press with your finger to mark the widths of the brick bands on either side of the dormer. At the places you have marked, make a 1cm cut with scissors, as far as the fold. Fold the central part back, leaving a return 0.5cm wide. This folded-back central part forms the windowsill. The two end sections, 1.2cm wide, are trimmed to a height of 1cm and glued to the lower part of the brick facing. Glue the remaining part (0.5cm wide) to the inside of the gutter.

4 Patinate the roof and dormers as described on page 188. 'Dirty' the chimney with the ash from incense paper (papier d'Arménie).

TOP OF MAIN ROOF

1 Cut four triangular pieces of 1mm Bristol board as shown. Join together with gummed paper on the inside.

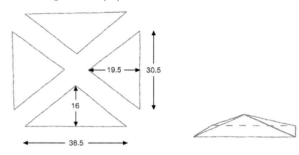

Take care!

If your house is to have electrical fittings, do not attach the top of the roof until all the interior fittings are in place (Chapter 2).

2 Glue the top to the main part of the roof, applying wood glue to the lower edge of each triangle. Paint to match the roof slates.

MAKING WINDOWS

1 The windows, which are fixed, are fitted between the edges of the inside and outside window surrounds. Each window comprises two large casements; those on the ground floor front have an additional light above (transom light or transom window). Each casement is made from:

• four long pieces of 2 x 5mm stripwood
• four short pieces of 2 x 5mm
• two long pieces of 2 x 2mm
• one short piece of 2 x 2mm.

The method is the same for all windows; only the dimensions vary.

2 First make a rectangular frame of 2 x 5mm stripwood. Then, using wood glue, stick 2 x 2mm battens to three sides of the frame, beginning with the short section at the base. Now make a second 2 x 5mm frame and glue this to the 2 x 2mm battens. You now have a frame (a casement) grooved to accept your window glass. Each window comprises two such frames.

3 Glue the two casements side by side. On the inside of the window, at the junction between the two casements, use wood glue to attach a 1 x 5mm strip: 12cm long for the ground-floor and first-floor windows, 4cm for the transom lights over the ground-floor doors and windows and 10.5cm for the dormers.

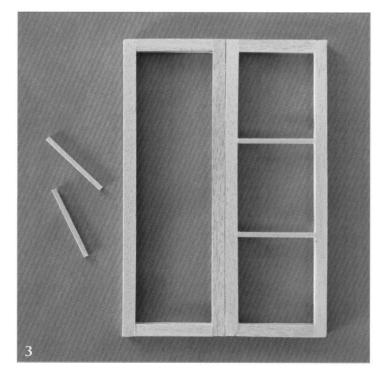

4 Gesso the whole assembly (including the insides of the grooves), without building up too much thickness. Paint off-white. Sand lightly to simulate wear. Apply patina no. 1 (page 188).

5 Cut window glass from thin acetate and slide this into the grooved frame. Install the window in the opening against the edges of the stone and brick window surrounds. Add finishing touches.

DORMER WINDOWS

- Overall dimensions: 6 x 10.5cm; each casement: 3 x 10.5cm.
- Frame members (2 x 5mm) per casement: 10.5cm (make 4), 2 cm (make 4).
- Battens (2 x 2mm): 10.3cm (make 2), 3cm (make 1).
- Glass: 2.4 x 10cm.

NB: This list of materials is for a single casement, not a pair.

1 Cut out and assemble as shown.

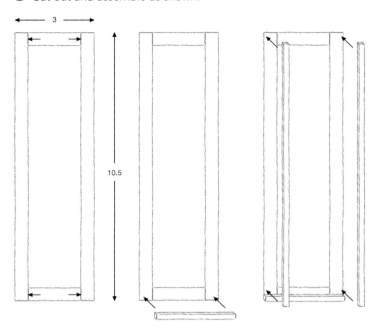

2 For the glazing bars, cut two 3cm lengths of 2 x 2mm batten. Glue the ends and place one bar 3cm from the top and the other 3cm from the bottom of the external frame.

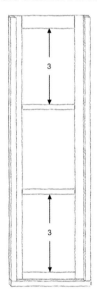

Note
Glue the roof on when all the internal decoration has been done.

GROUND-FLOOR WINDOWS

- Overall dimensions: 8 x 16.5cm; each casement: 4 x 12cm
- Frame members (2 x 5mm) per casement: 12cm (make 4), 3cm (make 4)
- Battens (2 x 2mm): 11.8cm (make 2), 4cm (make 1)
- Glass: 3.4 x 11.5cm
- Dimensions of transom (upper) window: 8 x 4cm
- Frame members for transom window (2 x 5mm): 8 cm (make 4), 3cm (make 8)
- Battens for transom window (2 x 2mm): 7.8cm (make 2), 4cm (make 1)
- Transom: 8.2cm of 5 x 10mm strip
- Glass for transom window: 7.5 x 3.4cm

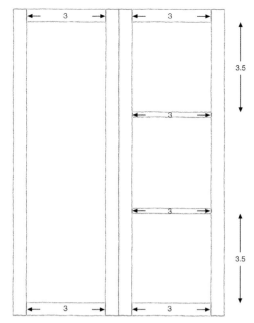

1 Glue the ends of the transom and set it into the notches in the window surround (page 19). For the transom window, make two frames to the dimensions given and assemble with battens between as before. In the centre, glue two 3cm lengths of 2 x 5mm strip, inside and out. Finish, glaze and glue in place.

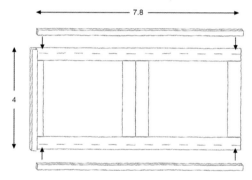

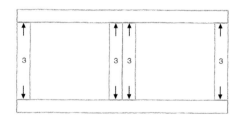

Transom

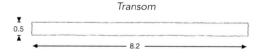

2 Make the two casements as before, adding 3cm glazing bars 3.5cm from the top and bottom, as you did for the dormer windows.

FIRST-FLOOR AND SIDE WINDOWS

- Overall dimensions: 8 x 12cm; each casement: 4 x 12cm
- Frame members (2 x 5mm) per casement: 12cm (make 4), 3cm (make 4)
- Battens (2 x 2cm): 11.8cm (make 2), 4cm (make 1)
- Glass: 3.4 x 11.5cm

1 Cut and assemble the parts according to the diagram. Add 2 x 2mm glazing bars as for the ground-floor windows.

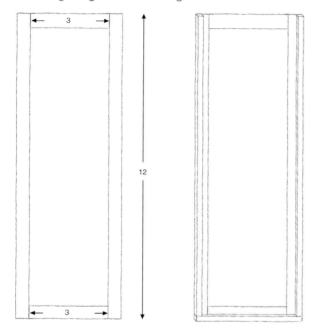

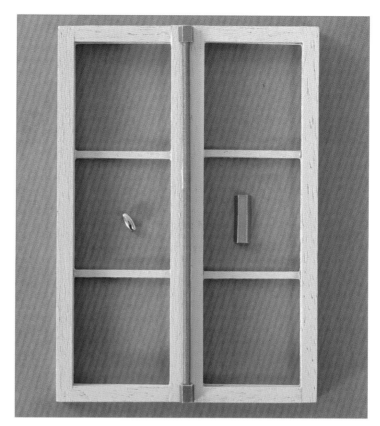

Lay the locking rod in position to check the length. Glue a length of 2 x 5mm stripwood over the joint between the casements. Glue the lock assembly to this strip.

WINDOW FITTINGS

1 With a utility knife, cut a 7mm strip of thin Bristol board. Score with the knife 2mm in from each of the long sides. Paint gold and leave to dry.

2 Cut a 2cm length of this to form the body of the door catch (crémone). Cut two 4mm lengths to represent the guides at each end of the locking rod.

3 For the locking rods, cut lengths of 2mm dowel: 12cm long for the casements, 4cm for the transom windows over the ground-floor windows and doors and 10.5cm for the dormer windows. Glue the rod to the strip that covers the joint between the two casements (page 30, step 3).

4 Fold back the edges of the gold-painted Bristol board where you have scored it. Glue the short sections to each end of the rod with wood glue. Place the larger piece halfway up. Superglue a small oval bead to this for the handle.

Note

The transom windows above the ground-floor casements also have locking rods. The short pieces of gold-painted Bristol board are added after the windows have been installed, to ensure that they are all aligned.

FRONT DOOR

- Overall dimensions: 21.4 x 8.4cm; each leaf: 16.9 x 4.2cm
- Frame members (2 x 10mm) for each leaf: 16.9cm (make 4), 2.2cm (make 2) + 2.2cm lengths of skirting (make 2). (Door frame is no. 1 in diagram overleaf.)
- 2 x 2mm batten (no. 2 in diagram): 16.7cm (make 2), 4.2cm (make 1)
- Glass for each door leaf: 11 x 3.5cm
- Lower panel (no. 3 in diagram): 2mm limewood, 3.5 x 5.5cm
- Middle rail (2 x 10mm) (no. 4 in diagram): 2.2cm (make 2)
- Transom (5 x 10mm): 8.6cm (make 1)
- Transom window frame (2 x 5mm): 8.6cm (make 4), 3cm (make 8)
- Transom window battens (2 x 2mm): 8.4cm (make 2), 4cm (make 1)
- Transom window glass: 3.5 x 8.2cm

1 Assemble the transom and transom window as for the ground-floor windows. When finished, glue into the opening in the front wall. Assemble the door as shown in the diagram.

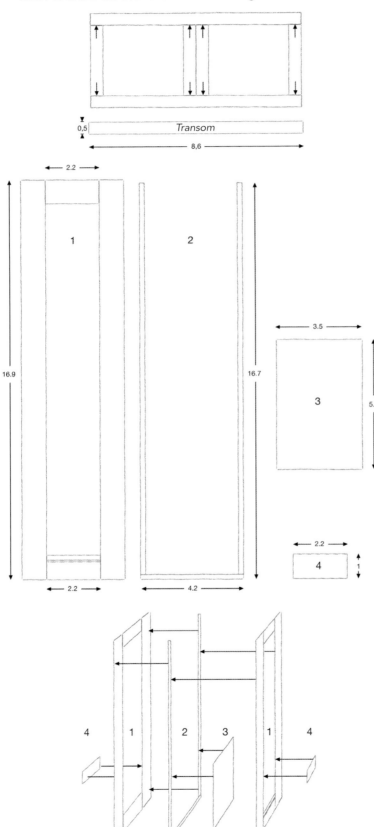

2 Cut a 16.9cm length of 2 x 5mm stripwood. Glue this over the joint between the two leaves of the door, on the inside.

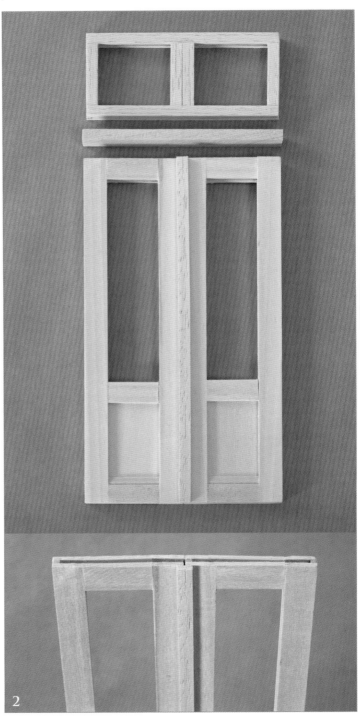

3 Coat with gesso, then paint the inside white. Paint the outside verdigris (equal parts of soft green and light grey), staying away from the grooves so as not to smudge onto the white side. Sand lightly to simulate wear. Apply a coat of tan and wipe off straight away. Sand lightly, then apply patina 1 (page 188) to both sides.

4 To simulate 'cathedral' glass, smear glue onto one side of the acetate. Spread and stipple this with your fingers to produce an irregular, granular appearance over the whole surface. Let it dry, then do the same on the other side.

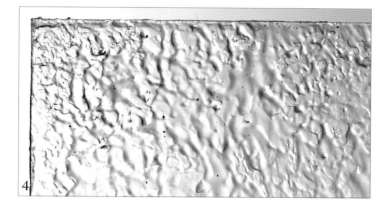

5 Slide the window glass into the wooden frames. Glue a gold-coloured bolt to the inside. On the outside, add a gilt-brass doorknob to one leaf of the door. Cut the lock plate, measuring 8 x 10mm, from thin Bristol board, painted gold. Glue this in place and use a compass point to pierce the keyhole.

6 Install the door in its opening so that it butts against the inside edges of the stone door surround.

SIDE DOOR

• Overall dimensions of door and frame: 19 x 7.6cm

1 This ready-made unit sits in the opening already prepared. Cut back the architrave with a utility knife as shown, so that the door sits within its surround.

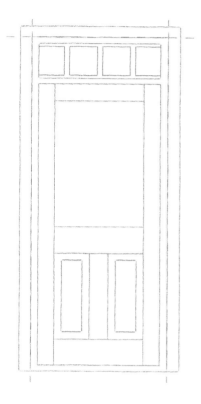

3 Using contact adhesive, glue the 0.5 x 0.5cm flat surface of the hinge to the upper side of the batten, 1.5cm from the top edge of the casement. Fold the excess back over the inside surface of the batten. Glue a second hinge to the lower end of the casement.

4 Glue the second frame to the battens. Paint, then insert glass.

5 Position the casement against the edge of the stone window surround, with the second frame facing you. You will see that the hinges, now that they have been inserted between the two frames, are not quite centred on the thickness of the window: they are closer to the frame which was fitted last. Installing the hinges as described should enable the window to open freely into the room.

6 On the inside of the house, where the walls have been built up with foamcore (see Chapter 2), fix the other flat part of the hinge (0.5 x 1cm) to the foamcore surround using solvent-free contact adhesive (solvent may damage the foamcore).

7 Cut a panel from thin Bristol board to fit the wall surface below the window (see page 60, step 6), but increase the height of this by 1cm. After painting, score lightly with a utility knife 1cm from the top. Fold back at a right angle, and glue down the folded part to form the inside windowsill.

8 Put a drop of glue on the 1cm flat part of each hinge. Using solvent-free contact adhesive, glue the moulded facings (see Chapter 2) into the window reveals, spreading the glue uniformly so that the hinges are sandwiched between the wall and the facing.

9 You can reinforce the assembly with nails no more than 3mm long, driven into the battens of the casements and into the walls. This method is suitable for internal doors also.

2 To remove the glazing in order to paint the door, slide the blade of a utility knife into the joints between the uprights and the top rail and detach the latter. Passing the blade around both sides will make it easier to detach the top rail and will prevent the wood from splintering in the process. Once the top rail has been removed, slide out the glass and paint the door with straw-yellow acrylic. Age the paintwork by sanding, as for the windows. Apply patina 1 (page 188).

OPENING WINDOWS

1 If you want your windows to be hinged, the height and width of the casement need to be slightly reduced to provide clearance. The overall width is reduced by 4mm, that is, at least 2mm for each casement, compared to the fixed windows. The height is also reduced by 2mm. So, for the front windows, the 2 x 5mm strips that make up the two frames of a casement will measure 11.8 and 2.8cm (make 4 of each). The battens will come to 11.6 (make 2) and 3.8cm (make 1). The hinges are then fitted *after* the battens have been glued to the first frame but *before* the second frame is glued to the battens.

2 To fabricate your own hinges, cut two strips 0.5 x 2cm from thick metal foil. Wrap the two strips around a 1cm length of florists' wire, leaving 0.5cm of the strip flat on one side and 1cm on the other.

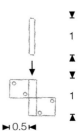

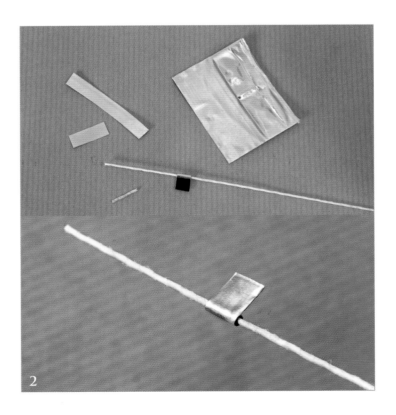

HOUSE STYLES

BELOW: BASTIDE. The front of this house shows all the hallmarks of the traditional Provençal farmhouse: a four-sloped roof covered with Mediterranean tiles (in Bristol board, painted to resemble terracotta) with a multiple row of tiles at the eaves (known as a génoise); windows taller than they are wide; dovecote windows at attic level; wooden front door in a stone surround of 18th-century character.

OPPOSITE: FLORIST'S HOUSE. The façade of this house is based on an abandoned 19th-century property in a Lorraine village, which once served as the local hospital. The façade, dormers and window surrounds resemble stone, with the wooden tiles painted to look like slate. Give or take a partition or two, the plans for this building are identical to the house described in this book.

ABOVE: DENTELLES ET RIBAMBELLES. This shop is reproduced in 1/12 scale to the millimetre, from the original in Montmartre, Paris. The model is all wood, with opening door and windows. The name of the shop means 'lace and paper friezes'; a ribambelle is one of those ornaments made by folding a strip of paper concertina-fashion and cutting out half a figure.

OPPOSITE: VETERINARY CLINIC. Inspired by a house near Honfleur in Normandy, the façade is coated with filler to imitate stone. Distinctive features include the slightly arched windows and the dormers entirely framed in red brick. The roof, in imitation slate, has skylights and a ventilator for the roof space. The wooden shopfront has a protective roof of zinc, a typical feature of old shops.

DECORATION

CEILING

Paint the ceiling matt white, including the edge of the stair opening and overlapping a little onto the floor of the landing. Use a gimlet to make the hole for the electric light fitting, positioned as shown.

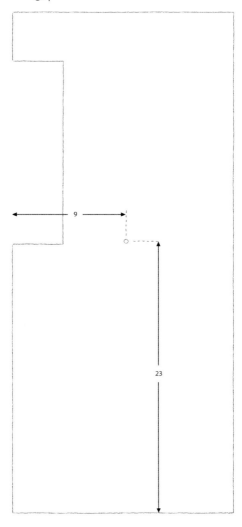

WALLS

1 Cut four strips 3.5 x 23cm (1) and one of 3.5 x 8.6cm (2) from 10mm foamcore. Attach strips 1 and 2 to the entrance wall as shown.

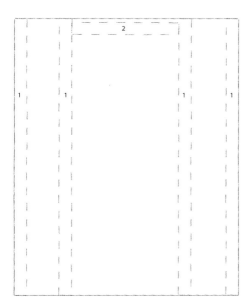

You will need

GENERAL
- Razor saw
- Small mitre box
- Utility knife
- Scissors
- 3mm gimlet
- Compass point
- Flat-nosed pliers
- Quick-setting wood glue
- Superglue (cyanoacrylate)
- 000 steel wool
- Medium and fine glasspaper
- Sponge
- Masking tape
- Paintbrushes
- Gesso
- Filler

CEILING AND WALLS
- 10mm foamcore
- 5mm foamcore
- 1mm Bristol board
- Cornice
- 13mm skirting
- 2 x 10mm limewood strip
- Ready-made semiglazed door and frame, 7.6 x 19cm
- Satin-finish acrylic paints:
    white
    ivory
- Matt acrylic paint:
    white

FLOOR
- 1mm Bristol board
- Squared paper
- Grouting cement, grey
- Satin-finish acrylic varnish
- Liquid wax polish
- Satin-finish acrylic paints:
    cream
    black

STAIRS
- 2mm balsa
- 1mm Bristol board
- 1.5mm florists' wire
- 30cm of braid
- Wooden banister (to make the newel post)
- 9mm wooden bead
- Acrylic woodstain: antique wood
- Modelmakers' paint or satin-finish acrylics:
    white
    light grey

2 Cut out a piece of 5mm foamcore 18 x 23cm to fit against the entrance wall. Cut out the opening for the front door. Glue this piece to the foamcore strips already fitted.

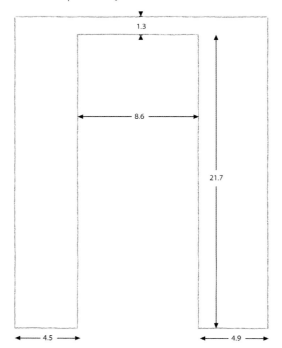

3 Mask off a 13mm strip along the bottom where the skirting will go. Do the same around the edge of the ceiling (except for the staircase opening, which will have no cornice), either side of the door opening (1cm wide) and around the kitchen door (0.5cm

wide). Coat the walls with filler. Remove the masking tape before the filler is completely dry. When dry, apply a coat of ivory satin-finish acrylic to all the walls; in the stairwell, overlap a little onto the wall of the room above.

CORNICE

Cut an 11.5cm length of cornice for the entrance wall, mitring the ends. For the right-hand wall, mitre the left end of the cornice and cut to fit, leaving the other end square. Paint matt white. Glue the cornice in place. Leave the left-hand wall for now.

FLOOR

1 Cut a paper template to the dimensions given in the diagram. Cut a 20 x 40cm rectangle and a 2 x 40cm strip from 1mm Bristol board. Paint the rectangle cream and the strip black.

2 Cut 144 large cream tiles and 162 small black ones. To speed up the process, cut one 'master' tile first. Cut a 2cm strip from the cream rectangle. Place your master tile on the end of this strip and hold it there firmly while you cut out the shape with scissors. Do the same along the whole length of the strip; if your scissors are good, you can even lay one strip over another and cut out two tiles at a time, provided you don't let the strips move. For the small black tiles, cut the Bristol board into 5mm strips, then cut again into squares. Paint the edges of both sets of tiles.

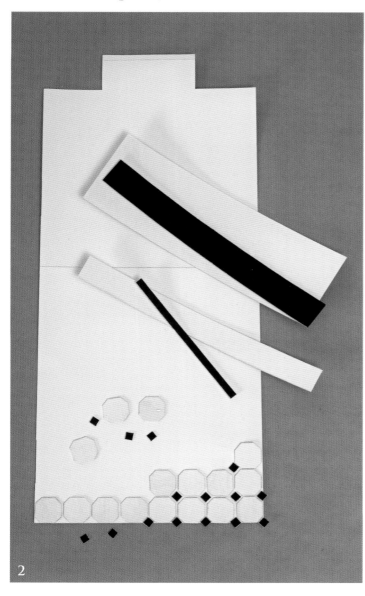

3 Lay the large and small tiles on the template as shown. Allowing for the joints, the cream tiles cover the floor exactly and do not need to be cut at the edges. Apply glue to the template as you go. Place the work under weights for half an hour or so to improve adhesion. Trim the edges, then spread glue on the underside of the template and glue it to the floor of the entrance hall. Use a heavy weight to keep it flat.

4 Varnish the tiles to protect them during grouting. When dry, spread grouting cement over the whole surface to fill the gaps. Wipe off the surplus with a damp sponge before it is completely dry. Wax, then buff gently with steel wool.

FRONT DOOR SURROUND

Cut the sides and top of the door opening from Bristol board. Score and fold as in the diagram. Paint white, including the scored lines and the edges. When dry, glue in position.

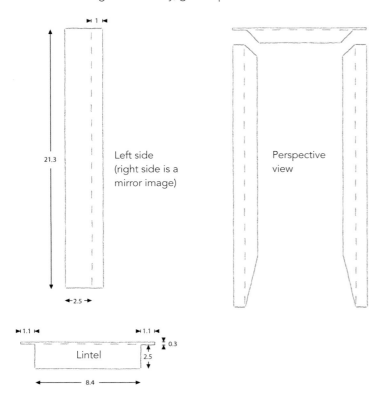

Left side
(right side is a
mirror image)

Perspective
view

SKIRTING AND KITCHEN DOOR

For the entrance wall, cut a 3.9cm length of skirting mitred on the right-hand end, and a 3.5cm length mitred on the left. For the right-hand wall, cut one length of 27.9cm, mitred on the left end. Paint and glue on; the skirting ends 5mm short of the kitchen door to allow for the architrave. Stain the ready-made kitchen door and frame, then glue in position.

STAIRCASE

1 The staircase structure is made from Bristol board, and the steps from 2mm balsa. The banisters are wire, and the handrail is made of Bristol board covered with braid.

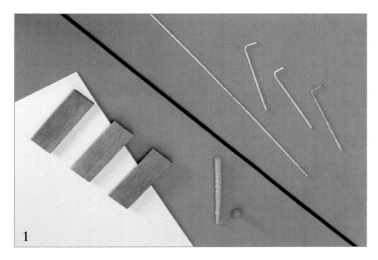

Cut the two stringers (side members; no. 1 in the diagram opposite) from Bristol board to the dimensions given. The height of the risers (no. 2 in the diagram) is 1.8cm and the surface on which the steps rest (no. 3) is 1.9cm wide. Measuring 1cm from each of these surfaces, make holes with a compass point in the right-hand stringer to receive the wire banisters.

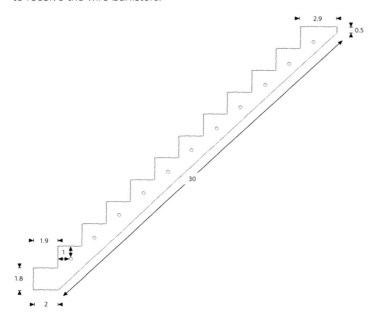

2 From Bristol board cut eleven risers 1.8 x 5.7cm, and a rectangle 5.7 x 30cm for the underside of the stairs (no. 4). Cut eleven steps from 2 x 6mm balsa. Lightly sand the front and right edges with fine glasspaper. Use glasspaper wrapped around a pen to hollow the centre of each step slightly. Stain the steps on both sides to prevent warping. When dry, buff with wire wool.

3 Lay out the two stringers facing you, the one with the holes on the right. Keeping them parallel, glue the first riser as shown. Put a dab of glue on each of the upright edges of the stringers. Fix the risers in place, taking care to form neat corners. Use masking tape to hold them in place. Leave to dry for an hour. Glue the stringers to the panel that closes the underside of the stairs, keeping the corners neat. Secure with masking tape and leave to dry.

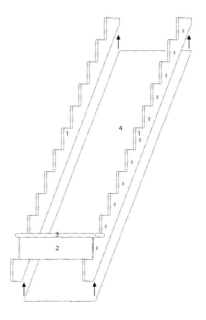

4 Cut the lowest riser from Bristol board and score lightly where indicated. Curve the section to the right of the score mark by wrapping it around a large felt-tip. Glue the straight part to the front edges of the stringers, then glue the curved part to the side of the staircase.

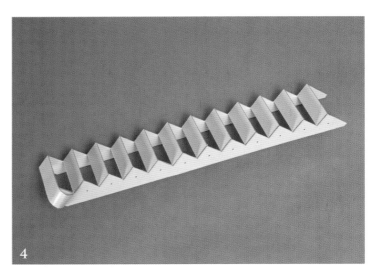

5 When dry, apply one coat of gesso to the whole structure, then paint satin white. Cut the lowest step from balsa as shown; finish to match the other steps.

6 Attach the steps one by one, applying glue to the edges of the stringers and risers; only the right-hand end of the step, with its rounded edges, overhangs by a few millimetres. Lay the staircase in its intended place against the wall and trace round the steps in pencil, then remove the staircase. Cut a 12.5cm length of skirting. Paint it satin white then glue it in place, setting the end of it flush with the rear edge of the wall.

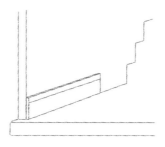

7 Glue edge to edge a piece of skirting and a piece of 2 x 10mm limewood strip, at least 30cm long. Reinforce the joint with masking tape on the back. Cut to length as indicated. Apply a little filler to the joint. Paint satin white.

8 Glue this piece to the wall, butting it against the skirting already in place, and following the pencil marks on the wall. Cut a 3cm length of skirting and glue this horizontally along the side of the top step. The staircase rests against this. Set one last section of skirting above the last balsa step.

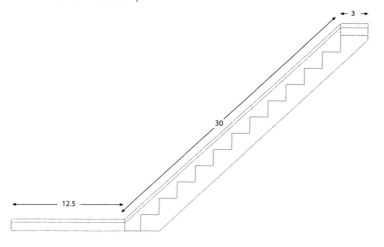

BANISTERS AND HANDRAIL

1 Cut a 6cm length of ready-made banister to make the newel post. Paint this light grey. Set it 1cm in from the edge of the bottom step, as follows: stick a pin into the step, then pull it out and insert it into the base of the newel post. Drive it in about 5mm, then cut it so that no more than 5mm is left sticking out. Dip the pin and the base of the post into a drop of wood glue, then insert the pin into the hole you made in the step. Apply pressure until the glue has begun to set. Wipe off excess glue immediately.

2 Cut eleven 7cm lengths of wire. Bend back the last 1cm of each piece using flat-nosed pliers.

Cut two identical handrails, 29 x 0.5cm, from Bristol board as shown. In one of them, pierce eleven holes with a compass point at intervals of 2.5cm. In each of these holes, place the straight end of one of the banisters, with a drop of superglue on the end. The bent ends of the wire must face inwards.

3 Check that the assembly is solid. Glue the second piece of Bristol board on top of the first. Add the braid along the top, stopping short about 1.5cm from the bottom end to allow for the knob; cut the other end to fit.

4 When all the parts are in place, apply a thin coat of gesso all over, then paint light grey. Finish with patina 1 (page 188). Glue the staircase in place. Attach the banisters and handrail by applying superglue to the bent ends of the banisters and inserting them into the holes in the stringer.

5 Paint the bead gold. Drive a pin, cut to a length of 1.5cm, through both thicknesses of Bristol board and about 6mm into the top of the newel post. Apply wood glue to the protruding end of the pin. Push the bead into the glue, pressing down slightly, removing any excess glue as you do so.

FINISHING TOUCHES

Cut lengths of wooden cornice to fit around the stair opening and along the left-hand wall, mitring the ends as needed. Attach the light fitting (see landing floor, page 76).

ENTRANCE HALLS

BELOW: FAMILY HOUSE. Provençal inspiration for the white walls with carvings and mouldings in Louis XV style. The floor is from real terracotta tiles.

ABOVE AND OPPOSITE: VETERINARY CLINIC. *The noticeboard was photographed at a real vet's surgery. Each notice was cut out and repositioned to match the original. The chairs are made of metal wire and Bristol board.*

You will need

GENERAL
- Utility knife
- Scissors
- Hole punch
- 3mm gimlet
- Hammer
- Dressmaking pins
- Quick-setting wood glue
- Wallpaper paste
- Masking tape
- Paintbrushes
- Sponge
- Gesso
- Filler

WALLS
- 5mm foamcore
- 10mm foamcore

WALL DECOR
- 1mm Bristol board or limewood sheet
- Thin Bristol board
- 2 x 10mm and 2 x 5mm limewood strip
- 3mm limewood sheet
- Wooden cornice
- 5mm dado rail
- Moulded dado rail
- 13mm skirting
- Wallpaper
- White imitation tile paper
- Satin-finish acrylic paints:
    cream
    soft green

COOKER HOOD
- 1mm Plexiglass
- 10 x 10mm stripwood
- Acrylic stain: light oak
- Glass paint: yellow

FLOOR
- 1mm Bristol board
- Squared paper
- Satin-finish acrylic varnish
- Grouting cement, grey
- Liquid wax polish
- Satin-finish acrylic paints:
    caramel
    off-white
    burgundy
    chestnut brown

CEILING
- 10mm balsa
- Matt acrylic paint:
    white

CEILING

Paint the ceiling matt white. The beams will be added later.

FRONT WALL

1 To build up the thickness of the front wall, cut the following pieces from 10mm foamcore: four vertical battens 2 x 23cm; two horizontal battens 2 x 8.2cm; and a large panel, 29.5 x 23cm, exactly matching the front wall. Cut one batten 2 x 23cm from 5mm foamcore. Cut out the window openings in the large piece, extending them right down to the floor. Cut two panels of 10mm foamcore, 5 x 8.2cm, to fit below the windows. The windows themselves will occupy 0.5cm of wall thickness; they are set in 1cm from the outside and 2cm from the inside.

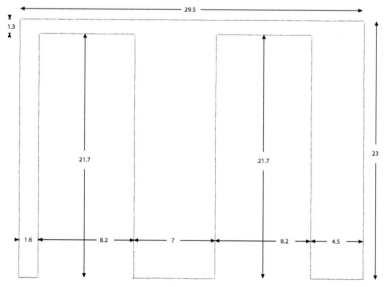

2 Glue on the battens, then the large panel and the panels below the windows. The idea is to build up the wall thickness to make the architecture and the window reveals more realistic.

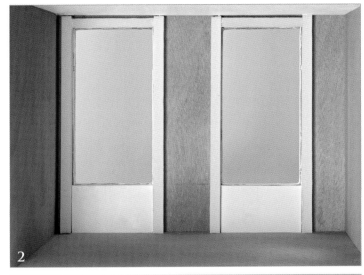

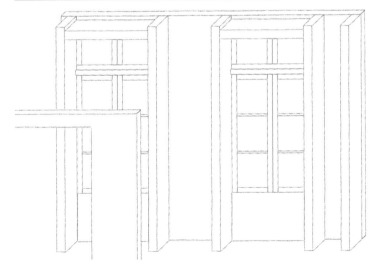

WINDOW REVEALS

1 For each side, cut a 2 x 21.7cm strip of thin Bristol board. Glue a 2cm length of 13mm skirting at the bottom; one end of the skirting must be mitred to meet the skirting which will be placed below the window.

2 Cut a 2 x 20.4cm strip of 1mm Bristol board. Cut out an opening 1.4 x 19.4cm, leaving a margin of 0.3cm on the long sides and 0.5cm on the ends. Glue this piece to the first piece above the skirting.

3 Cut the remaining relief pieces from 1mm Bristol board to the dimensions shown. The circular and semicircular cuts are made with a hole punch.

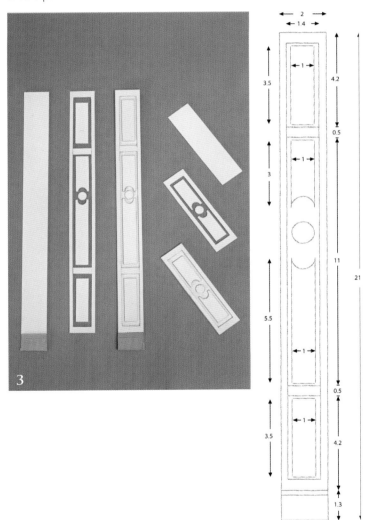

4 Make two identical panels for each window, remembering that the skirting must be mitred on the end facing the window. Coat with gesso, then paint cream. Now set these pieces aside.

5 For the soffit (top panel), cut a 7.8 x 2cm strip of thin Bristol board. Cut a second strip the same size from 1mm Bristol board, and cut out the centre as before. Add reliefs and paint as for the sides, following the dimensions below.

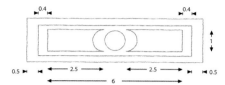

6 For the dado panel below the window, cut a 5 x 8.2cm rectangle from thin Bristol board. Glue on an 8cm length of skirting, mitred at both ends; centre this on the bottom part of the dado panel, leaving a 1mm gap either side. Finish to match the side pieces (reveals), then glue in position. Now glue the soffit and reveals into place. Finish by adding 8cm dado mouldings, painted to match, below the windows.

WOODWORK AND WALLPAPER FOR FRONT WALL

Each element of the wall decoration is laid out on a template of thin Bristol board. It's important to set these out in the right order: front wall, then left wall, and finally right wall.

1 Cut out the template for the front wall, allowing for the thickness of the relief panels already installed.

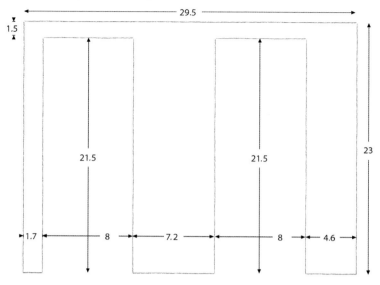

2 Glue the various parts onto this template following the numbers in the diagram below. The dado rail and skirting are cut to fit.

- 1: 2 x 10mm limewood strip, 26.3cm long
- 2: 2 x 10mm limewood strip, 22cm long
- 2a: 2 x 5mm limewood strip, 22cm long
- 2b: 2 x 10mm limewood strip, 5.2cm long, placed 6.5cm up from floor level
- 3: 13mm skirting
- 4: Dado rail
- 5: Dado rail cut in two lengthwise, mitred at corners
- 6: 1mm Bristol board or limewood sheet, 3 x 4cm

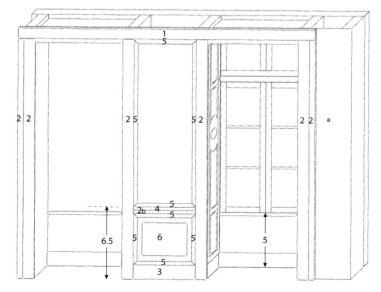

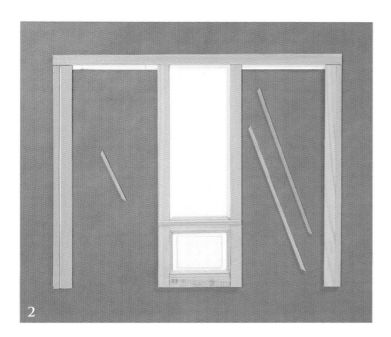

2

3 Cut out the centre of the template by running the blade of the utility knife along the halved dado mouldings surrounding the upper panel, where the wallpaper is to go. Lay the template on the wall and trace round this opening in pencil. Coat the template and attached woodwork with gesso, then paint cream.

3

4 Cut a 5 x 16cm strip of wallpaper. Paste, then place it between the windows in the space you have marked. Now glue the template to the wall.

4

5 To finish, apply filler to all the joints between the wooden members and the background layer, smooth and wipe over with a damp sponge.

LEFT-HAND WALL

1 For the part that is decorated with wallpaper and panelling, proceed as before, using a template of thin Bristol board measuring 23 x 16.8cm. Glue on the parts following the numbered stages in the diagram. Cut the dado mouldings to fit.

- 1: 2 x 10mm limewood strip, 16.8cm long
- 2: 2 x 10mm limewood strip, 22cm long
- 2a: 2 x 10mm limewood strip, 14.8cm long, placed 6.5cm up
- 3: 13mm skirting, 14.8cm long
- 4: Dado rail, 16.8cm long
- 5: Dado cut in two lengthwise, mitred at corners
- 6: 1mm Bristol board or limewood sheet, 3 x 13.3cm

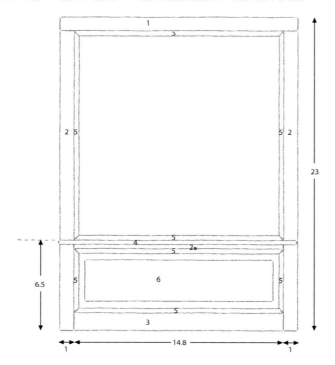

2 The boarded section of the wall is made from 2 x 10mm limewood strips and a single piece of 2 x 5mm. On a 23 x 21.2cm template of thin Bristol board, mark the position of the door by pressing with your finger around the edges of the opening. Turn the template over and cut from the back along the lines you have marked. Glue on the skirting. Spread a thin coat of wood glue on the template. Lay the wooden strips side by side, beginning with the one to the right of the door. Continue to the right-hand end, then work back towards the left end. Place the work under weights from time to time as you proceed. Trim the ends.

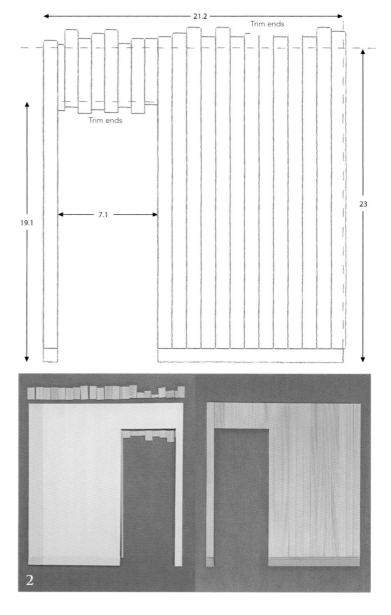

3 If any gap appears between the ready-made door frame and the wall, cut three lengths of 2 x 5mm limewood strip to serve as an architrave.

RIGHT-HAND WALL

1 Before attaching any battens, mark a line 19.2cm up from the base of the wall to indicate the height of the horizontal battens.

2 Cut parts from foamcore as follows:

From 5mm foamcore:
- 1: Two battens 2 x 23cm

From 10mm foamcore:
- 2: Four battens 2 x 23cm
- 2a: One batten 2 x 20.2cm (this one should stop short of the ceiling to provide space for electrical wiring coming down from the upper floors)
- 3: One batten 2 x 5.2cm
- 4: One batten 2 x 8.2cm
- 4a: One batten 2 x 8cm

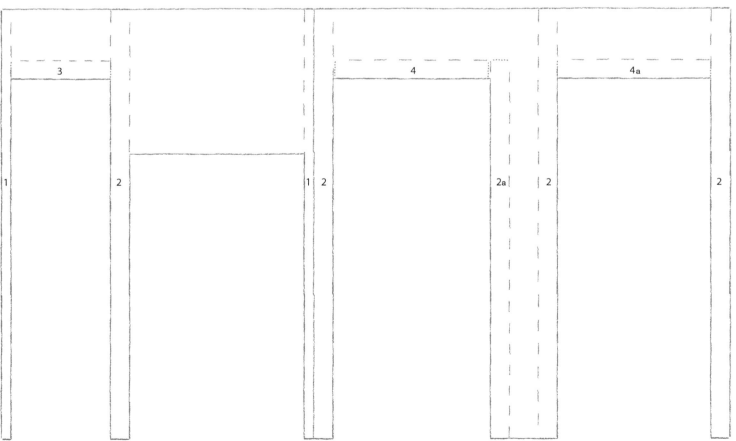

3 Cut a large panel of 10mm foamcore as shown. Fix this to the battens with wood glue.

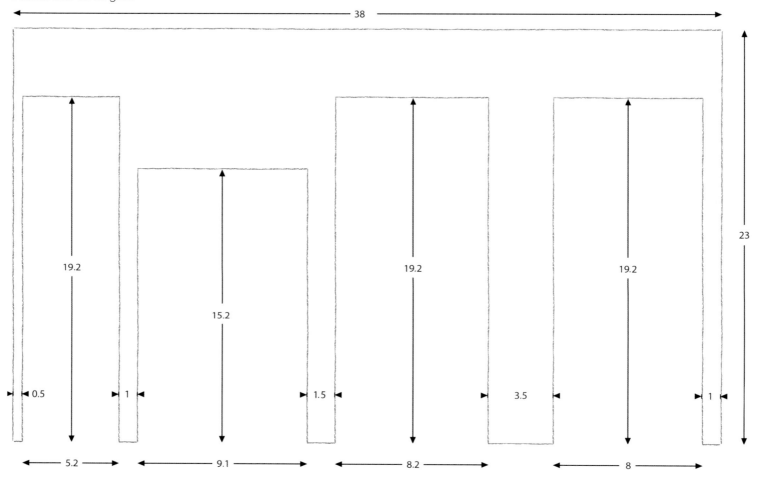

38

23

19.2

15.2

19.2

19.2

0.5

1

1.5

3.5

1

5.2

9.1

8.2

8

3

4 Cut pieces of 1mm Bristol board to line the recesses.

- Shelf/fridge recess: 1 piece 3 x 5cm, 2 pieces 3 x 19.2cm
- Cooker recess: 2 pieces 3 x 15.2cm
- Sink recess: 1 piece 3 x 8cm, 2 pieces 3 x 19.2cm
- Door surround: 1 piece 3 x 7.8cm, 2 pieces 3 x 19.2cm

5 Glue the pieces of Bristol board into the recesses to neaten the edges. Apply a coat of filler to the insides of the recesses, except those for the sink and cooker. Leave to dry.

5

6 Place masking tape so that its lower edge is 7.5cm from the floor. Paint the lower part of the wall sea-green (equal parts cream and soft green). Remove the tape, leave to dry, then mask the green part while you paint the upper part cream.

7 Cut two shelves 3 x 5cm from 3mm limewood sheet. Paint cream, trim if necessary, then glue them into the fridge recess at 10.7 and 15.7cm from the floor.

8 Line the sides and top of the sink recess with imitation tile paper: two strips 3 x 13cm and one 3 x 8cm. Line the back and sides of the cooker recess similarly, using two strips 3 x 15cm and one strip 8.9 x 15cm.

COOKER HOOD

1 Cut a rectangle of Plexiglass measuring 3 x 8.9cm (the length may have to be adjusted depending on the thickness of the filler in the cooker recess). Give it a smoked-glass effect as you did for the front door (page 35, step 4). If you want to tint the glass, paint it beforehand with glass paint, on one side or both depending on the shade desired. Glue in place at the top of the cooker recess.

2 Cut a 10cm beam from 10 x 10mm stripwood. Apply a light oak stain. Glue it to the wall above the glass panel using wood glue.

Tip

To reinforce the beam, cut the heads off two dressmaking pins and dip them in wood glue. Using pliers, push them in at an angle (one a mirror image of the other) through the beam and into the foamcore.

FINISHING THE CEILING

1 Drill a hole with a 3mm gimlet through the floor of the living room above, 17cm from the right-hand side and 14cm from the front edge. Cut a groove in the living-room floor leading from this hole to the opening you made for the wires to go through.

2 Cut the beams from 10mm balsa to the widths given below; adjust the lengths to fit.

- 1: one beam 2 x 1cm
- 2: four joists 0.5 x 0.5cm
- 3 and 3a: eight beams 1 x 1cm

Tip

To make the 0.5 x 0.5mm joists, cut a strip 5mm wide from 10mm balsa, then cut this strip in half.

3 For greater realism, chamfer the edges with the utility knife, and distress the surface by hammering and scratching. Paint cream. Stick the beams with wood glue in their proper places, beginning with beam 1; keep the spacing regular. Coat with filler as you did for the walls and wodwork.

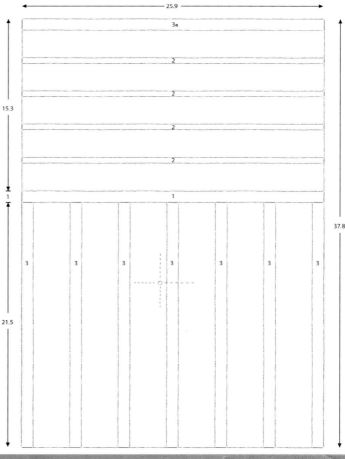

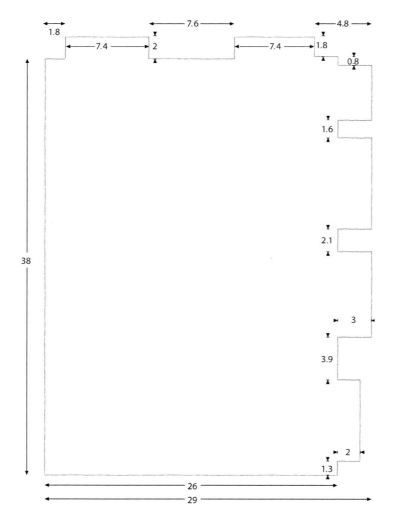

Note

Like a real house that has been modified over the years, this room combines a kitchen and a dining room that were once separated by a partition. The original rooms were arranged either side of a deep central beam. The treatment of the walls recalls the original layout.

Note

The tiles are cut and fitted along the walls as in a real house. If the floor is laid before building up the walls, the heights of the wall linings would have to be reduced by about 2mm, and a hole drilled in the tiles for the electrical wires.

FLOOR

1 Cut a template from squared paper to the exact dimensions of the floor (29 x 40cm), following the diagram below.

2 Cut about 800 hexagonal tiles from 1mm Bristol board to the pattern shown. Speed the work by using the method described for the entrance hall (page 47, step 2). Glue the pieces to the template by spreading on wood glue a little at a time. Leave to dry under weights. Turn over the template and trim any overlapping tiles.

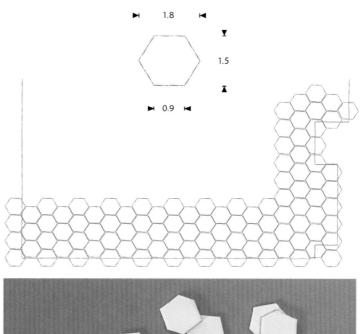

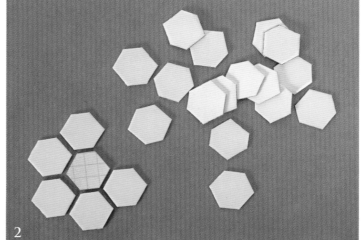

3 Coat with gesso, then colour terracotta as described on page 188. Varnish to protect the tiles during grouting. Glue the template to the kitchen floor and weight it down while it dries.

4 Apply masking tape to the skirting boards all round the room. Use grouting cement to fill all the gaps. Before this is fully set, wipe off the excess with a damp sponge. Allow to dry, then wax with a soft rag.

KITCHENS AND DINING ROOMS

Right: Bastide. The balsa floor imitates terracotta.

Opposite page and below: Château. The kitchen of this grand country house is huge but intimate, a place steeped in tradition and dominated by the big cast-iron stove. The flagstone floor is painted balsa.

Bottom, left and right: Family house. This kitchen is inspired by that of the novelist George Sand at Nohant in central France, but the layout has been modified to fit the limited space. The walls are plastered with filler, and the floor is covered with eggshell-coloured tiles in real terracotta.

The flaking walls, stone sink and painted beams give this room a country feel.

The food safe is made from limewood, the food from air-drying clay.

TOP, LEFT AND RIGHT: VETERINARY CLINIC. The floor is an imitation of hexagonal terracotta tiles. It was actually made with real tiles glued to a sheet of Bristol board, and then photocopied to save weight, since the house was intended to be easily transportable. The arched windows are hinged to open.

ABOVE: CHALET. The mixture of materials – brick, stone, wood – gives this room its authentic character.

RIGHT: BASTIDE. The glazed earthenware of the country pottery is simulated with paint and varnish. The stone sink was once a drinking trough for animals.

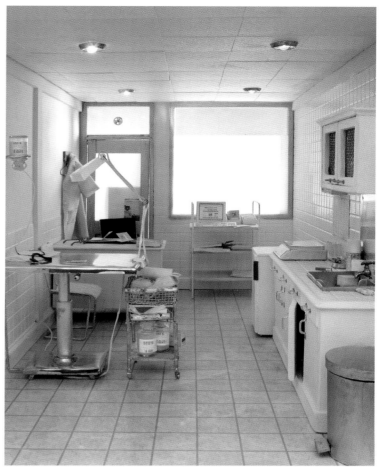

ABOVE: A HOUSE IN THE COUNTRY. This is decorated in a Nordic style, achieving a warm effect with 'cold' colours. The floor is made of terracotta tiles framed by lengths of stained limewood.

RIGHT AND BELOW: VETERINARY CLINIC. The imitation marble floor is a commercial product made of paper. All the furniture is made from wood, Bristol board, paper or metal. Syringes, stethoscope, patient records, drugs compendium and other accessories are all copied from the originals.

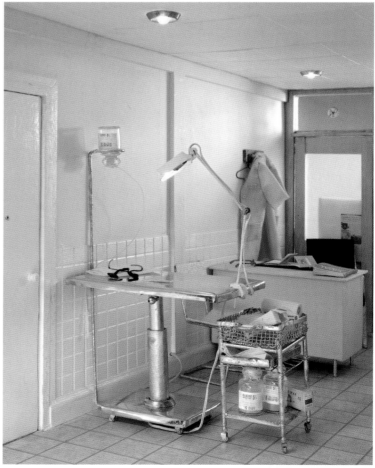

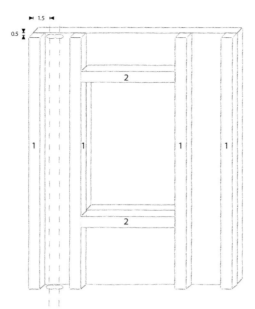

Note

The landing must be completed before installing the partition that separates it from the bathroom. Since it will be visible only through the window or the bathroom door, the materials used to decorate it are simplified – the floor, in particular.

CEILING

Paint the ceiling matt white, then pierce a hole for the light fitting. The beams will be added later.

WALLS

1 From 5mm foamcore, cut out a panel to the same dimensions as the wall, and the following battens:
1: Four battens 1 x 23cm
2: Two battens 1 x 8.2cm.
Glue the battens to the wall as shown, fixing the 1cm face to the wall: this wall will be thinner than the others. Glue the foamcore panel to the battens.

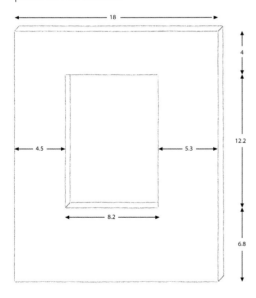

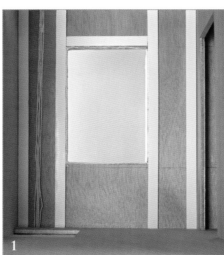

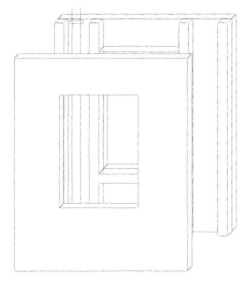

You will need

GENERAL
- Wood glue
- Utility knife
- 3mm gimlet
- Minidrill and 3mm bit
- Masking tape
- Compass point
- Flat-nosed pliers
- Quick-setting wood glue
- Superglue (cyanoacrylate)
- Gesso
- Sponge
- 000 steel wool
- Medium and fine glasspaper

WALLS
- 5mm foamcore
- 1mm Bristol board
- 1 x 5mm limewood strip
- Filler
- Satin-finish acrylic paints:
  ivory
  tan
  cream

STAIRCASE
- 2mm balsa
- 1mm Bristol board
- 1.5mm florists' wire
- 30cm of braid
- Satin-finish acrylic paints:
  white
  light grey
- Acrylic woodstain: antique wood
- One wooden banister
- Filler

FLOOR
- Imitation tile paper

CEILING
- 10mm balsa
- Matt acrylic paint:
  white

2 Apply masking tape to make a 0.5cm border around the window and door openings. Apply filler, then remove the tape before the filler has dried. Leave to dry.

3 On each of the side walls, draw a vertical line 18cm from the front wall to indicate the position of the bathroom partition. Lay masking type along this line (on the bathroom side) to prevent the filler from spreading too far. Apply filler, then paint all the walls with a mixture of ivory and tan.

4 For the window surround, cut two pieces of 1 x 5mm limewood strip 13.2cm long, and two more 9.2cm long. Mitre the ends.

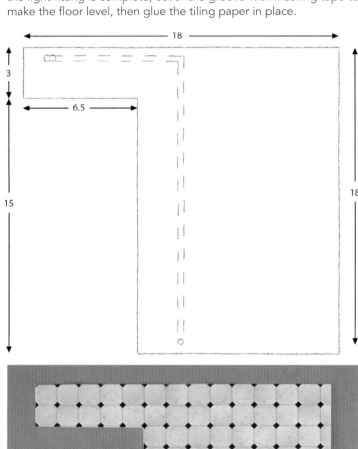

It's up to you whether you decorate the wall and window surround in situ, or laid flat on your work surface (in which case you will have to touch up the filler and paint after assembly).

FLOOR

Cut out the imitation tiling paper as shown. Before laying the tiling paper, make a groove with a minidrill and 3mm bit to take the electrical wire for the light fitting in the entrance hall. Attach the light fitting, lay the wire in the groove, then bring it down to the basement through the conduit made in the entrance wall of the hallway (see page 10 and photos on pages 45 and 46). Once the installation of the light fitting is complete, cover the groove with masking tape to make the floor level, then glue the tiling paper in place.

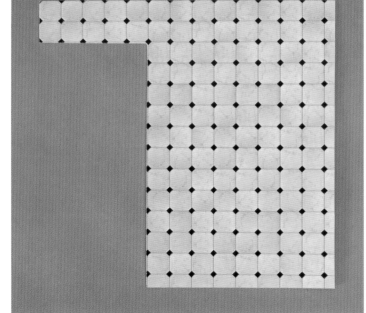

Beams

Cut a groove in the floor of the nursery above to house the wire for the light fitting. Attach the light fitting. Cut the beams from balsa to the dimensions given. Treat them like those in the kitchen, then stain them an oak colour and place them as shown.

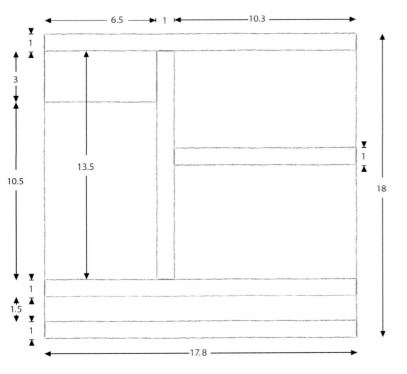

Staircase

1 The dimensions of the steps and risers on this staircase are not quite the same as for the ground-floor stairs, because of the limited space on the landing. Cut two stringers from 1mm Bristol board for each section of this angled staircase. As before, there is no need to drill holes for banisters in the side that will be glued to the wall.

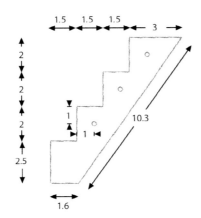

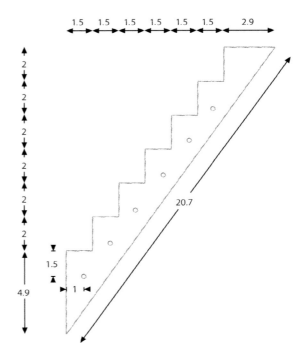

2 Cut a rectangle 4.8 x 21cm from 1mm Bristol board for the underside of the second flight of stairs (the first flight is left open underneath) and cut six risers measuring 2 x 4.8cm.

Cut the half-landing from 2mm balsa. The part that sticks out will be the right-hand end of the fourth step.

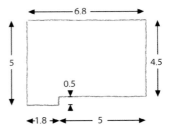

3 Cut eight steps from 2 x 5mm balsa. Treat them in the same way as those on the ground-floor stairs. The first step and its curved riser are made like those on the ground floor, to the dimensions indicated.

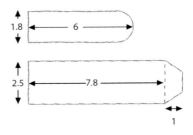

4 Following the diagram, assemble the staircase in the same order as the ground-floor one. Paint in the same way.

5 The top of the staircase is glued to the first-floor ceiling.

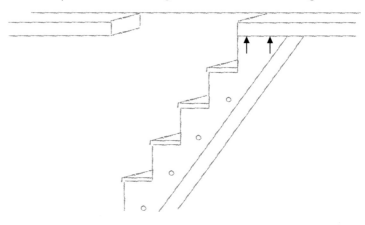

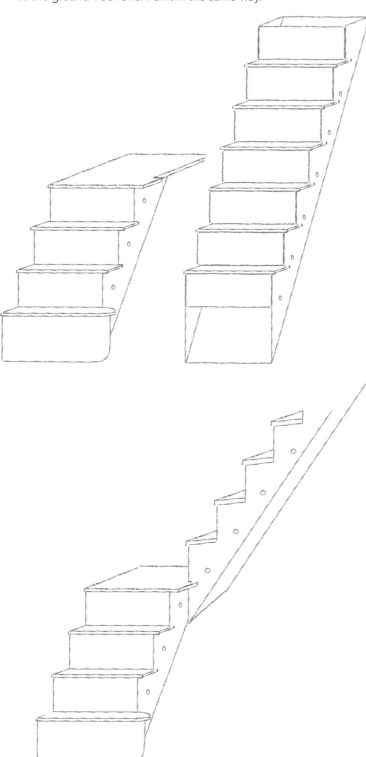

BANISTERS AND HANDRAIL

The handrail is made in the same way and from the same materials as that of the ground-floor stairs. It must follow the angle of the stairs and continue up to the second floor to make a safety railing in the nursery.

1 For the railing of the first-floor landing, cut two pieces as shown from 1mm Bristol board. In one, drill six holes at intervals of 1.5cm from the straight end. Cut the banisters 5.5cm long and attach them to the handrail as before. Assemble the handrail, paint and apply patina as before.

2 Fit the railing so that its curved end meets the straight end of the handrail coming up from the ground floor.

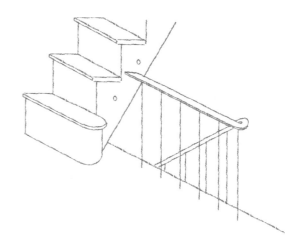

3 Cut two pieces as shown from 1mm Bristol board. Drill holes for banisters in one of them.

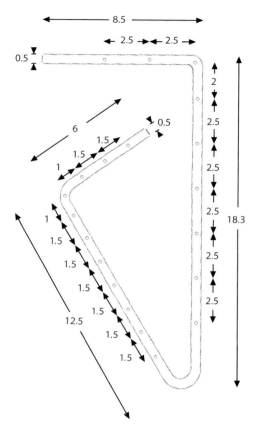

4 Cut eleven 6cm lengths of wire for the safety railing on the second floor; set these aside for now.

5 Install the newel post in the same way as you did on the ground floor (as before, this is a wooden banister 6.7cm long, painted light grey). Cut three pieces of wire 8.5cm long for the lower run of banisters, and six more 7cm long for the upper part, plus one piece 5cm long which will go into the last hole of the handrail and into the first hole in the nursery floor. Bend the wires as before, except those for the top section. Attach the banisters and handrail as before, but leave the second-floor railing for now: it will be fixed to the nursery floor once the floor covering is in place.

CEILING

Paint the ceiling matt white. The beams will be added later.

LEFT WALL

Cut a rectangle 21.5 x 23cm from imitation tile paper. Coat the back evenly with wallpaper paste. Fold it over and leave to soak for 5–10 minutes. Glue in place, squeezing out the air bubbles.

FAR WALL

1 On the 18 x 23cm partition (see page 14), draw a circle as shown and cut it out with the fretsaw. Cut out the door opening below the round window. Cut glazing bars from 2 x 2mm limewood and adjust to fit. Glue them in place, then gesso both sides of the partition. Paint the bathroom side of the wall satin white.

2 Cut a rectangle 6.2 x 5.9cm from 1mm Bristol board and cut out the centre to make a frame 5mm wide to surround the circular window. Paint satin white.

3 Cut a door 6 x 15.6cm from limewood sheet. Cut 2 x 5mm battens as shown. Trap the hinges beneath one of the battens (see page 36). Cut the dado moulding in half lengthwise to reduce its width. Cut it to fit around the panels as shown in the diagram overleaf; mitre the corners.

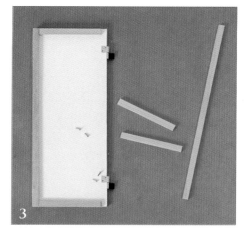

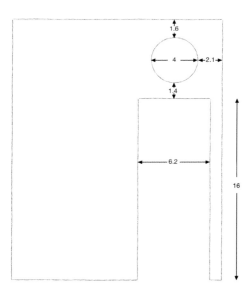

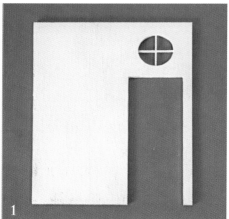

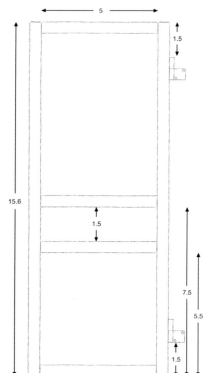

GENERAL
- Fretsaw
- Utility knife
- Scissors
- Compass point
- 3mm gimlet
- Hammer
- Coarse and fine glasspaper
- Wallpaper paste
- Wood glue
- Superglue (cyanoacrylate)
- Paintbrushes
- Masking tape
- Gesso
- Filler

WALLS AND INTERIOR DOOR
- Thin Bristol board
- 1mm Bristol board
- 3mm limewood sheet
- 2 x 2, 2 x 5 and 2 x 10mm limewood strip
- Dado rail
- 1.5mm florists' wire
- Thick metal foil
- 3mm mini-nails
- Imitation white tile paper
- Filler
- Satin-finish acrylic paints:
    cream
    white

FLOOR
- Squared paper or thin Bristol board
- 3mm balsa
- Satin-finish acrylic varnish
- Grouting cement, grey
- Liquid wax polish
- Satin-finish acrylic paint:
    white

CEILING
- 10mm balsa
- Matt acrylic paint:
    white

5 Cut the right-hand side of the architrave from 2 x 5mm limewood according to the diagram. The heights of the two notches must match those of the hinges. Cut the left side from 2 x 10mm lime. Paint satin white and assemble.

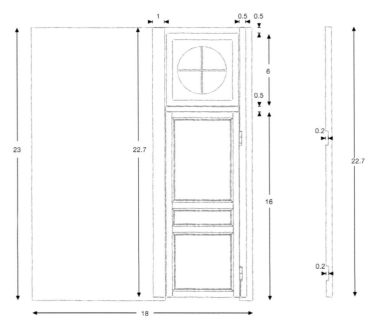

4 Cut out the relief panels from 1mm Bristol board and glue them to the door; these measure 4 x 4, 0.5 x 4 and 6 x 4cm. Decorate the other side of the door in the same way (the hinges are on one side only). Paint satin white.

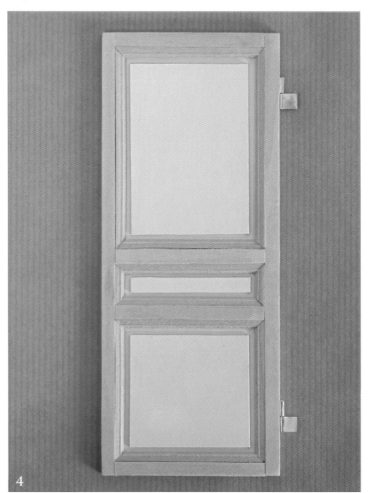

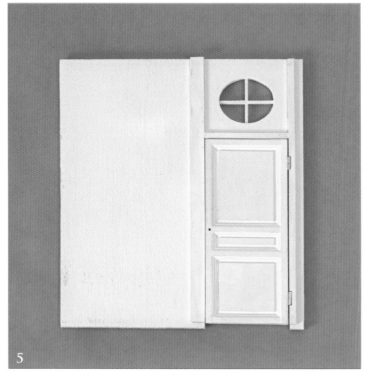

6 Finish the dado area with imitation tile paper measuring 9.6 x 9.2cm.

LANDING SIDE OF THE PARTITION

1 Mask off the door on three sides. Paint the circular window cream, taking care not to spread onto the bathroom side. Leave to dry. Mask off the area around the circular window. Apply filler to the wall. Paint. Cut the square and circular window surrounds from 1mm Bristol board. Paint to match the other landing wall. Glue in place.

2 Glue the partition up against the staircase and the beam on the landing ceiling. Insert a spacer if need be to keep the partition plumb.

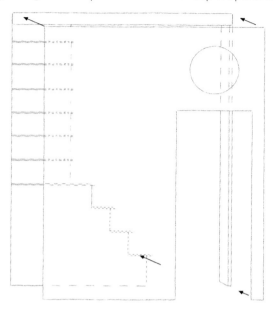

RIGHT-HAND WALL

1 Cut a template 21.5 x 22.9cm from thin Bristol board. Paint with gesso. Allow to dry completely, so the Bristol board becomes stiff. Cover the Bristol board with the stencil, allowing an overhang of 1–2cm to make it easier to hold. Spread a 1–2mm layer of filler over the stencil. Remove the stencil immediately, and leave to dry.

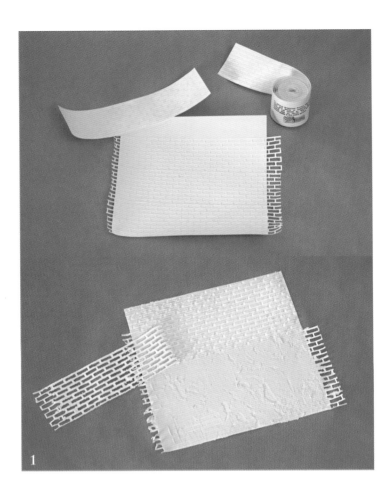

Note

The adhesive stencil can be used to make imitation stone or brick walls (see the chalet, florist's house and veterinary clinic, pages 110, 108 and 72).

Tip

If some of your tiles break under pressure, reassemble them as you lay them to create thoroughly realistic cracks.

2 Paint the tiles with gesso on both sides, so they do not warp. When completely dry, paint them satin white.

3 Glue the tiles to the template, leaving 2mm between them. Cut off the parts that overhang. Varnish the tiles, then glue the template to the bathroom floor. Grout and finish as for the kitchen floor.

FINISHING THE CEILING

1 Drill the hole for the light fitting. Cut four beams from 10mm balsa. Treat them like those in the kitchen. Paint matt white and glue in position. Thread the wire for the light fitting through the hole. Lay the wire into the groove you have already cut in the floor of the nursery above (see page 76). Attach the wires to the strings you prepared for them. Cover the groove with masking tape. Pull the wires down into the basment.

STONE-EFFECT FLOOR

1 Cut a template 18 x 21.5cm from paper or thin Bristol board. Cut 80 tiles 2 x 2cm from 3mm balsa. Round over the edges with sandpaper. Place the tiles upside down on a sheet of coarse glasspaper, or some other rough and irregular surface. Tap each tile with a hammer, varying the force of the blows, so it takes on the roughness of the surface underneath and begins to look like stone (balsa is a very soft wood).

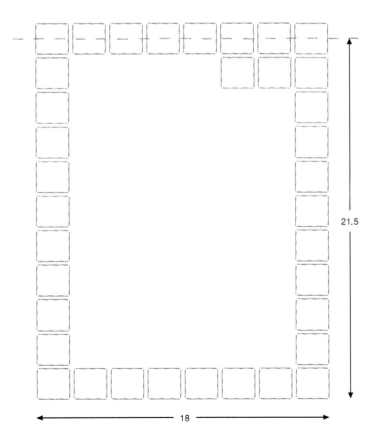

BATHROOMS AND LAUNDRY ROOMS

BELOW: FLORIST'S HOUSE. The shabby-chic bathroom is entirely clad in wooden boards painted with a single coat of white acrylic, wiped off in places to give an aged look.

OPPOSITE: BASTIDE. Placing the bath on a raised wooden platform is an attractive design feature in a room short of space.

ABOVE: *FLORIST'S HOUSE. The linen room in the attic boasts ample storage. With a washing machine at the back, the whole area serves as a laundry.*

OPPOSITE: *FAMILY HOUSE. In this early 20th-century bathroom the walls have small glass tiles up to the dado rail. The washstand has been custom-made to fit a porcelain washbasin, and fitted with a brass towel rail.*

You will need

GENERAL
- Utility knife
- Hole punch
- Compass point
- 3mm masonry bit
- 5mm gimlet
- Quick-setting wood glue
- Contact or mastic adhesive
- Fine glasspaper
- 000 steel wool (optional)
- Paintbrushes
- Gesso
- Filler

WALLS
- 10mm foamcore
- 5mm foamcore

WALL DECOR
- 2 x 10mm limewood strip
- 1mm Bristol board or limewood
- Thin Bristol board
- 5mm dado rail
- 13mm skirting
- 10mm wooden cornice
- Satin-finish acrylic paints:
    off-white
    light grey
    cream

CEILING
- 9cm ceiling rose in resin
- Matt acrylic paint:
    white

FLOOR
- Thin squared paper
- 2mm limewood sheet
- 2 x 10mm limewood strip
- 2 x 5mm limewood strip
- Woodstain: light oak
- Liquid wax polish

DOOR
- Ready-made double door and frame
- Satin-finish acrylic paint:
    off-white

HEARTHSTONE
- 2mm limewood sheet

CEILING

Paint the ceiling and rose with a coat of matt white. Make a hole with the gimlet 14.7cm from the right-hand side and 19cm from the near edge to accommodate the wire for the light fitting. Drill through the centre of the rose with the masonry bit. Pass a temporary string through the holes in both ceiling and rose. Fix the rose to the ceiling with contact cement or with mastic (which fills any gaps just like a filler). Apply a second coat of paint all over.

VERSAILLES PARQUET

1 Enlarge the template below to the required dimensions (8 x 8cm). Make 15 photocopies and cut them out.

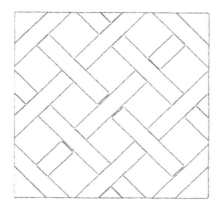

2 Stain the 2mm limewood sheet on both sides to prevent warping.

Note

It's possible to stain the parquet after laying it, but if there is any trace of glue on the surface the stain will not take.

3 Cut a strip 1.2cm wide from the stained limewood sheet. Cut this into 12 squares (no. 1 in the diagram). From the same sheet, cut a strip 0.6cm wide. Cut this into 13 lengths of 3.1cm (no. 2), four of 1.2cm (no. 3) and four pieces 0.6cm square (no. 5). From the same sheet, cut a strip 0.8cm wide and cut this into four lengths of 1.8cm (no. 4). Use a paintbrush to stain the edges. Fix the pieces to the template with wood glue as shown.

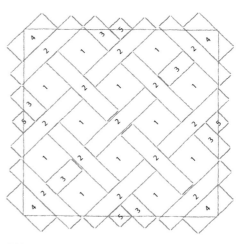

4 Weight the assembly until dry, then sand with fine glasspaper.

5 When all the pieces have been laid, trim the edges with the utility knife to produce a 7 x 7cm square with neat, square corners.

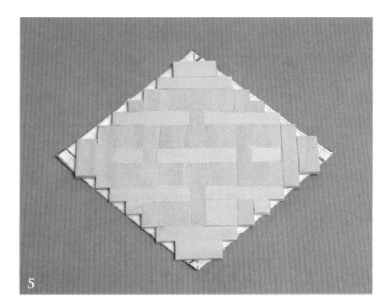

6 Spread glue evenly on the back and glue to a piece of thin paper. Cut a 0.5cm strip from the stained limewood. From this cut four lengths of 7.5cm (no. 6) and glue these in place as in the diagram.

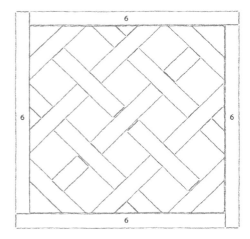

7 Cut off the excess paper all round and trim the edges with the utility knife to make an 8cm square (no. 1 in the diagram at right). Place under weights. Make 15 panels in this way.

8 Cut a template for the whole floor from thin paper, measuring 28.5 x 35cm. On the right-hand side, cut out a rectangle 6.5 x 11.5cm, starting 13.5cm from the far wall; this is for the hearth.

9 Cut five of the panels diagonally (no. 2 in the diagram at bottom).

10 Glue the panels to the template as shown, then cut out the opening for the hearth (dotted lines). Cut the leftover half-panel into two quarters and glue these into the corners.

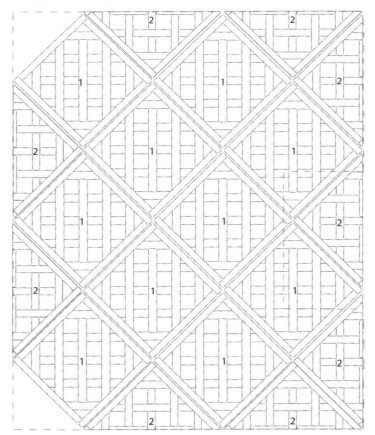

11 Stain the floor again and wax it. Rub over with 000 wire wool to give an aged effect.

Note

You may have to make adjustments to the last two quarter-squares. If they are too small, make a whole new square and cut this into halves, then quarters, to finish the corners of the parquet floor.

Tip

When cutting a narrow strip which does not run the full length of the wood, cut the ends first (across the grain) to prevent the wood from splitting further than you intended.

12 Glue the parquet to the floor, leaving a margin of 0.5cm on either side and 1cm along the near edge. Fill the gaps with 2mm limewood strips cut to the appropriate width. Lay five strips 1cm wide along the far end. With a utility knife, cut out a recess in the left-hand strip to accommodate the door sill (below, left). Lay three strips around the hearth (below, centre).

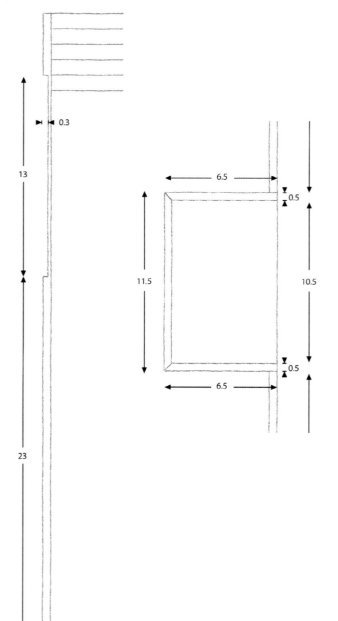

HEARTHSTONE

Cut out a rectangle 5.9 x 10.4cm from 3mm limewood sheet. Paint all over with gesso, then paint in imitation marble (see page 188). Cut a notch 1cm square at the back edge for the electrical wires, then glue to the floor.

DOOR

Install the ready-made door and frame, painted off-white, with the architrave facing the landing; apply glue to the architrave and the sill. Make sure that the door sill butts up against the recess you cut in the floor, and that the architrave fits snugly against the landing side of the wall. On the inside of the room, replace the architrave with plain strips of 2 x 5mm lime.

FAR WALL

1 From 10mm foamcore, cut five battens 2 x 22.7cm, two battens 2 x 8.2cm and a wall panel to the dimensions given below.

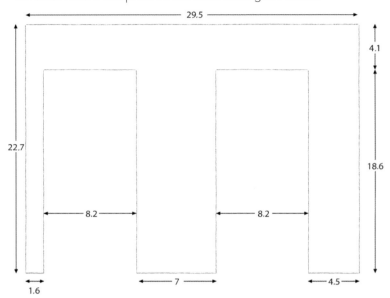

2 From the same material, cut two dado panels 6.5 x 8.2cm to fit below the windows. Glue the battens, dadoes and wall panel into position.

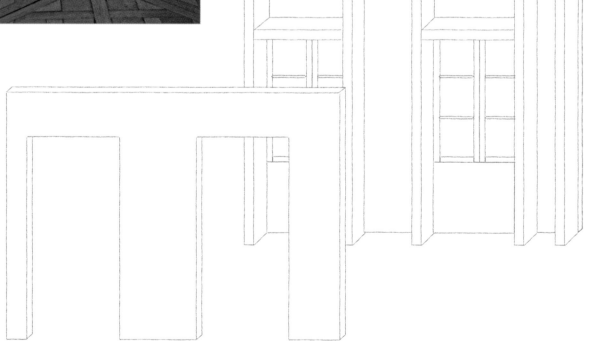

3 Make the window reveals and soffits as you did for the kitchen, following the diagrams. Gesso the backgrounds and paint them cream, then paint the raised panels pearl-grey (equal parts cream and light grey). Put aside for now.

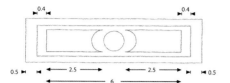

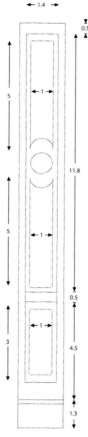

4 Cut two pieces of thin Bristol board the same size as the dado panels and finish them with skirting as in the kitchen. Paint with gesso, then pearl-grey, and glue in place below the windows. Below each window, fit a length of dado moulding, gessoed then painted cream. Glue the reveals and soffits in place.

5 Cut a template from thin Bristol board for the wood panelling.

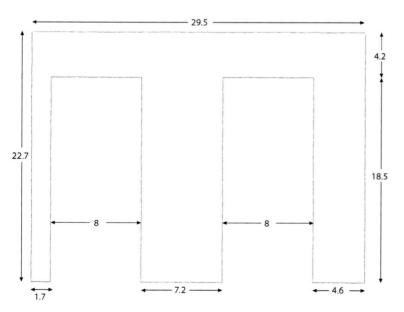

6 Paint all the parts pearl-grey except nos. 5, 5a, 6, 7 and 7a, which are cream. Attach the strips and panels in numerical order. Cut one section of dado rail into two lengthwise; this forms the moulding inside the panels enclosed by strips 1, 3, and 3a.

- 1: 2 x 10mm limewood strip, 21.7cm long
- 2: 13mm skirting (baseboard), 5.2cm long
- 2a: 13mm skirting, 2.6cm long
- 3: 2 x 10mm limewood strip, 2.6cm long
- 3a: 2 x 10mm limewood strip, 2.5cm long
- 4: 1mm Bristol board or lime, 3 x 3.5cm
- 4a: 1mm Bristol board or lime, 1 x 3cm
- 5: 1mm Bristol board or lime, 3.5 x 12.5cm
- 5a: 1mm Bristol board or lime, 1 x 12.5cm
- 6: Dado moulding cut in half lengthwise; cut to fit and mitre the ends
- 7: Whole dado moulding, 7.2cm long
- 7a: Whole dado moulding, 4.6cm long, mitred at right

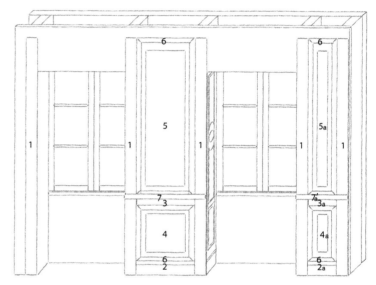

7 Glue the template to the wall. Paint a length of cornice matt white and cut to 29.5cm. Mitre both ends to meet the cornices on the side walls. Glue in place.

LEFT-HAND WALL

1 Cut a template from thin Bristol board for the wood panelling.

2 Use the same method as for the far wall; only the measurements are different. The overdoor panel is left smooth.

- 1: 2 x 10mm limewood, 21.7cm long
- 2: 13mm skirting, 22cm long
- 3: 2 x 10mm lime, 20.4cm long
- 4: 2 x 10mm lime, 10cm long
- 4a: 2 x 10mm lime, 5cm long
- 5: 1mm Bristol board or lime, 3 x 8cm
- 5a: 1mm Bristol board or lime, 3 x 3.5cm
- 6: 1mm Bristol board or lime, 8 x 12.5cm
- 6a: 1mm Bristol board or lime, 3.5 x 12.5cm
- 7: Whole dado rail, 24cm long
- 8: Dado rail cut in half lengthwise; cut to fit and mitre the ends

3 Glue the template to the wall. Add a 29.5cm length of cornice painted matt white, mitred at the right-hand end and cut square at the other.

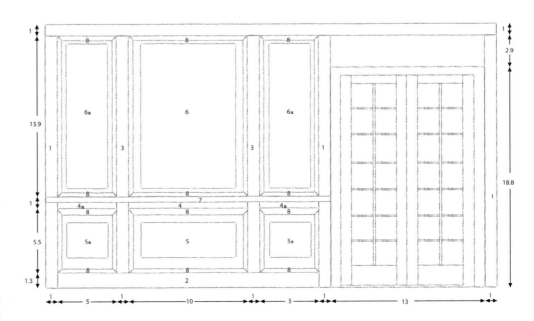

RIGHT-HAND WALL

1 Cut a template from thin Bristol board for the wooden panelling. Make two holes for the light fittings and an opening 3cm square centred on point A. This opening will prevent the wires for the light fittings from being trapped between wall and floor when the template is glued to the wall. It also allows you to retrieve the strings you put in earlier and attach them easily to the wires.

2 Proceed as for the other walls; only the dimensions are different. Don't glue the template to the wall until all the light fittings are in place.

- 1: 2 x 10mm lime, 21.7cm long
- 2: 13mm skirting, 10.8cm long
- 2a: 13mm skirting, 2cm long
- 2b: 13mm skirting, 7cm long
- 3: 2 x 10mm lime, 10.8cm long
- 3a: 2 x 10mm lime, 2cm long
- 3b: 2 x 10mm lime, 7cm long
- 4: 1mm Bristol board or lime, 3 x 9.3cm
- 4a: 1mm Bristol board or lime, 0.8 x 3cm
- 4b: 1mm Bristol board or lime, 3 x 5.5cm
- 5: Dado rail cut in half; cut to fit and mitre the ends
- 6: 1mm Bristol board or lime, 9.3 x 13.5cm
- 6a: 1mm Bristol board or lime, 0.8 x 13.5cm
- 6b: 1mm Bristol board or lime, 5.5 x 13.5cm
- 7: Whole dado rail, 15.8cm long
- 7a: Whole dado rail, 12cm long

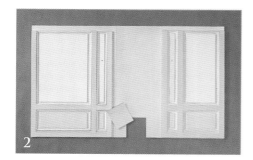

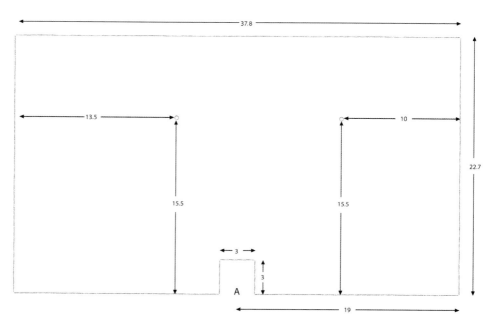

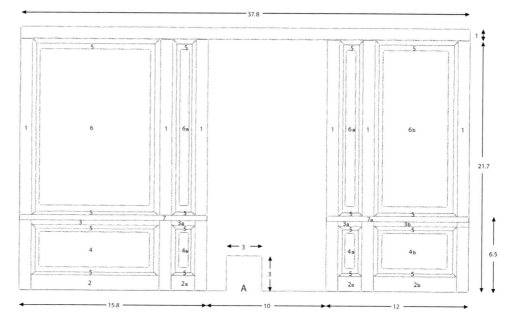

LIGHT FITTINGS

1 Attach the wire for the ceiling fitting to the string already in place in the rose so that you can bring it up through the ceiling. From the hole, cut a groove in the floor of the bedroom above as far as the notch in the ceiling that you made at the construction stage.

2 Pull on the string until the electric wire appears in the room above and the top of the light fitting is snug against the ceiling. There is no need to glue it; it will stay up by itself because the wire is held in the groove by the masking tape (as described on page 11).

3 Detach the temporary string from the electric wire and fasten the latter securely with masking tape to one of the strings placed earlier in the interior of the walls. Press the wire into the groove in the attic floor. Pull on the string from below until the wire from the light fitting appears in the basement; cover with masking tape.

4 Now position the wall fittings. Pierce two holes in the wood panelling to match those already made in the back of the wall template. Pass the wires through these. Cover the wires behind the template with masking tape, keeping them perfectly flat and bringing them to point A, which coincides with the hole made in the floor. Attach a string to each wire and bring them down to the basement. Leave some slack and set aside for the time being.

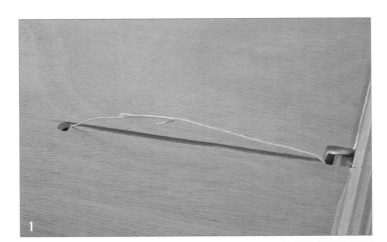

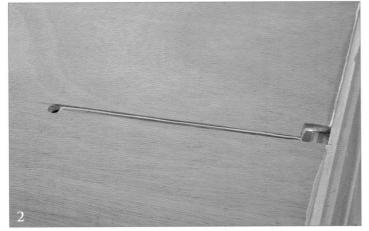

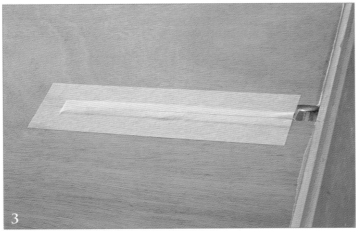

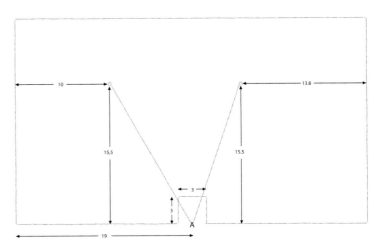

5 Cut a groove in the plywood wall at least 5mm wide to accommodate the wire from the ceiling fitting. The reason for the extra width is that it will also take the wire from the attic bedroom above; put in a string for this wire also. Cover with masking tape. Glue the template to the wall. Finish pulling the wires through.

FINAL TOUCHES

Paint the last length of cornice matt white and attach it. Fill any gaps between the mouldings and the ceiling with filler. Depending on the effect desired, apply patina 1 (page 188) or put another coat of matt white on the cornice, taking care not to get any on the panelling.

SALONS AND LIVING ROOMS

BELOW: CHÂTEAU. Panels of roses, gilded mouldings on a pinkish-beige background and an imitation-marble fireplace provide an appropriate setting for the harpsichord in the music room. The Chantilly parquet is made from strips of wood, stained then waxed, after an existing original.

OPPOSITE AND FOLLOWING SPREAD: The great baroque salon is the largest room in the château: 45cm wide by 65cm long, with a ceiling height of 31cm. The baroque ambience blends the elegance of Louis XV with the sobriety of Louis XVI. The restrained furnishings prevent it from looking overly ostentatious.

ABOVE AND TOP: FAMILY HOUSE. The largest room in the house is the grand Louis XVI reception room. The chevron-patterned parquet (known as point de Hongrie) is made from thin slips of wood.

LEFT: The wire-mesh door and tasselled key, the parquet in basketweave pattern and the painted furniture evoke a country-chic atmosphere inspired by the Gustavian style from 18th-century Sweden.

OPPOSITE PAGE: CHÂTEAU. In this eclectic boudoir a Louis XV fireplace and overmantel rub shoulders with Louis XVI bergère armchairs and a Venetian chest of drawers. The walls are covered with wood panelling in typically 18th-century green, tapestries and photocopied fabric panels. The light fitting has been given a shabby-chic makeover, with printed fabric and branches of ivy over a washed-out grey patina.

ABOVE AND OPPOSITE PAGE: FAMILY HOUSE. Printed fabric, wooden panels and restyled furniture and light fittings give a rococo look typical of the Louis XV period. Carpets, cushions and fire screen are hand-embroidered. The dining room beyond is largely inspired by that of the 19th-century playwright and poet Alfred de Musset; the decor has an 18th-century flavour.

LEFT: FLORIST'S HOUSE. The sitting room brings together all the favourite themes of a florist with a taste for antiques, such as painting, second-hand china, 18th-century fabrics, books and pictures… and, of course, an immoderate love of flowers, especially old roses.

Below and below right: Bastide. The furnishing of this living room is typically Provençal in style. The cushions and upholstery are made using photocopies of local fabrics.

Bottom: Chalet. The fireplace in imitation stone, the sofa and the dresser were all custom-made. The rest of the furniture is in natural wood, stained and waxed to match the warm tones of the real terracotta tiles on the floor and the wooden boarding on the walls.

Opposite page: A house in the country. The furniture is made from simple kits which, once they have been customized, allow the beginner to fit out a house at very little cost. The armchair has been re-covered with fabric, with cushions added to make it more comfortable. A panel in the back of the sofa has been cut out and replaced with a piece of canvas to resemble woven cane. Faded colours and gold braid complete the impression of Gustavian style softened by time. The light fitting is a reproduction of an early 20th-century design; the pâte de verre effect is achieved with a coat of pearl nail varnish and touches of other colours which blend together while they are still wet.

You will need

· GENERAL
- Fretsaw
- Utility knife
- 3mm gimlet
- Quick-setting wood glue
- Wallpaper paste
- Contact adhesive
- Dressmaking pins
- Paintbrushes
- Fine glasspaper
- 000 steel wool
- Gesso
- Filler

WALLS
- 10mm foamcore
- 1mm Bristol board
- Thin Bristol board
- 2 x 10mm limewood strip
- 3mm limewood sheet
- Wooden dado moulding
- 13mm skirting
- Cast resin swags for wall decoration
- Mirrored acetate
- Wallpaper
- Tulle (7 x 12cm)
- Cotton fabric (12 x 14cm)
- Satin-finish acrylic paint:
    cream
- Modelmaking paint:
    silver

CEILING
- 10mm balsa sheet
- Matt acrylic paint:
    white
    cream

FLOOR
- Squared paper
- 1 x 8mm limewood strip
- Acrylic woodstain: light oak
- Liquid wax polish for parquet

CEILING

1 Paint the ceiling (31.5 x 38.5cm) matt white on both sides. Since it is made from 1mm Bristol board, both sides must be painted to avoid warping as it dries. Do not glue.

POINT DE HONGRIE (CHEVRON) PARQUET

1 Cut two floor templates from squared paper. Template 1, representing the total floor area, measures 23.5 x 40.5cm; template 2, representing the area within the outer border, measures 20 x 37cm. The border, in theory, is 1.6cm wide (equal to two 0.8cm strips side by side). To allow for slight gaps between the border strips and the five central bands, we will assume an overall margin of 3.5cm. If, after assembly, the template turns out to be larger than intended, simply reduce the border by a few millimetres. The five central strips each measure 3.9 x 37cm.

2 Cut a strip of squared paper to the dimensions of one of the five main bands. Cut 32 pieces of 1 x 8mm lime, 8cm long. To save time, cut one piece first to use as a master, as for the tiles on the ground floor. Mitre the right-hand end of one piece; the others will be laid parallel to this first piece.

3 Apply glue evenly to about half the template. Lay the first piece as shown. Cover the whole template, spreading more glue as you go, then cut off the overhanging ends. Fill in the corners with offcuts. Make two more bands of diagonal parquet identical to this one. Weight the pieces down until dry.

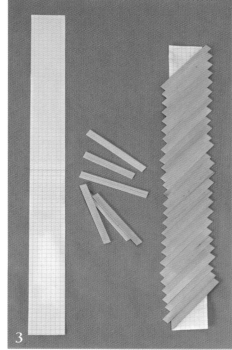

4 Make two more bands angled the opposite way.

5 Glue the five bands to template 2, carefully aligning the corners. Glue template 2 in the centre of template 1, ensuring an equal margin on all four sides. Glue on the border strips, cutting them to fit and mitring the corners.

6 Cut out the section where the fireplace will go. Cut a notch in the bottom left corner of the floor to accommodate a trim piece. Apply wood stain and finish before gluing template 1 to the floor.

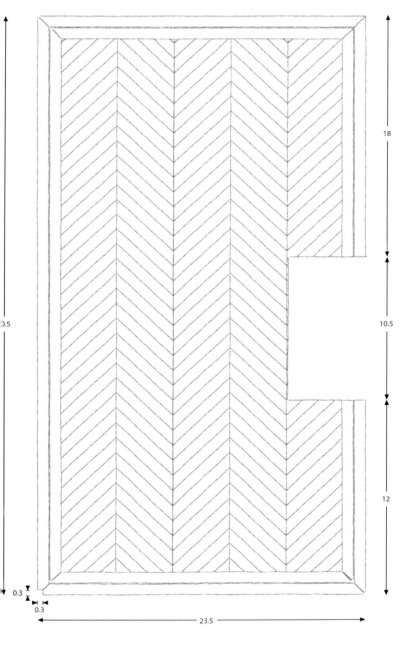

7 Assemble the parquet for the fireplace area from 1 x 8mm limewood strip on a template of squared paper, then glue it in place. Stain and finish as for the salon floor before gluing it into place.

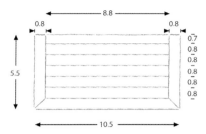

FAR WALL

1 Insert the windows into the dormers. Cut pieces of 1mm Bristol board as shown in the diagram. Gesso, then paint cream and glue into the window reveals and soffits. These pieces hold the windows in place.

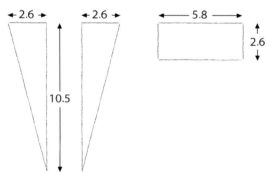

2 Cut the wall template from thin Bristol board. Angle the right-hand end to match the slope of the roof, and cut out the window openings.

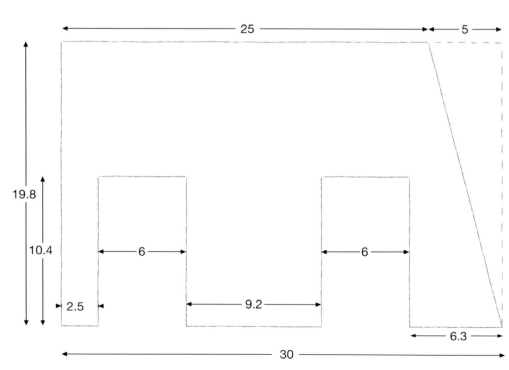

3 Attach wooden strips and skirting in the order shown. Gesso, then paint cream.

- 1: 2 x 10mm limewood, 23.5cm long
- 2: 2 x 10mm limewood, 18.8cm long
- 3: 2 x 5mm limewood, 6cm long
- 4: 13mm skirting, 7.2cm long

4 Cut strips of wallpaper to fit between and above the windows. Lay them in position, press with your finger to mark the exact positions of the frames, then trim with scissors before pasting the paper. Glue the template to the wall. Finish with filler, as in the other rooms.

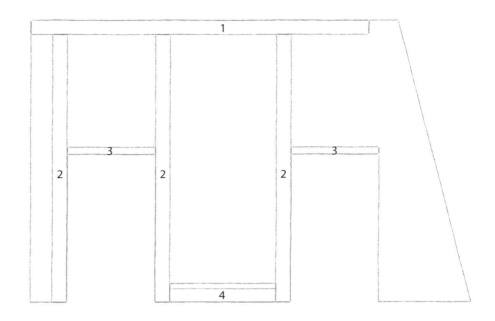

Left-hand wall

1 Cut a wall template from thin Bristol board. Angle both ends to match the slope of the roof, and cut out the door opening.

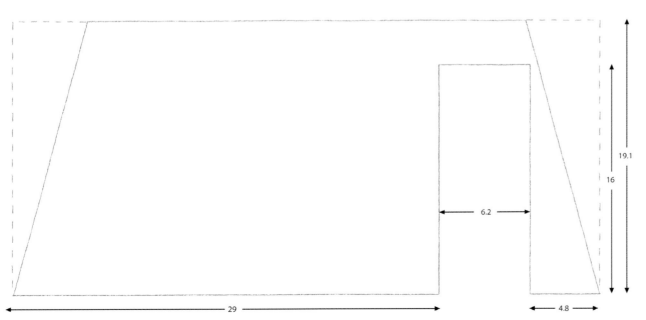

2 Glue on the door, limewood strips, dado rail and skirting in the order shown. Apply gesso, then paint cream.

- 1: Door identical to the bathroom door (see pages 81–2)
- 2: Dado moulding 0.5cm wide, cut to fit and mitred at ends
- 3: 13mm skirting, 28.5cm long
- 3a: 13mm skirting, 4.3cm long
- 4: Dado rail, 1 x 27.5cm (see Tip below)
- 4a: Dado rail, 1 x 3.3cm
- 5: Dado moulding, 0.5 x 13cm, mitred at ends
- 5a: Dado moulding, 0.5 x 12.5cm, cut to measure and mitred at ends

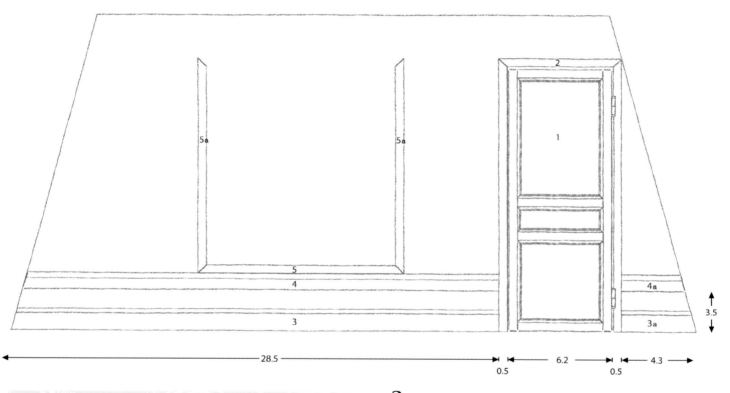

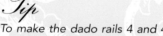

To make the dado rails 4 and 4a, glue a 0.5cm moulding to a 2 x 10mm limewood strip.

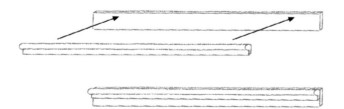

3 Paint the inside edge of the door surround cream. Paste wallpaper into the framed panel. Mitre the ends of the cast resin swag to fit the top of the frame; paint cream and glue in place. Glue the template to the wall. Finish with filler as usual.

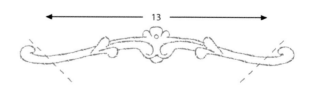

RIGHT-HAND WALL

1 Cut a wall panel from 10mm foamcore to the dimensions shown in the diagram.

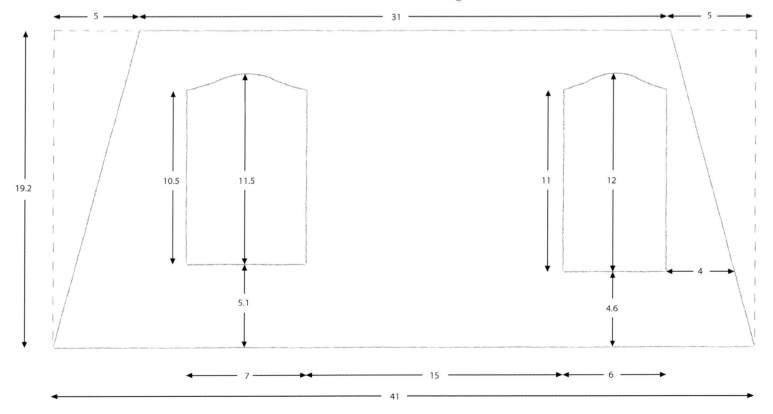

2 Cut the openings for the niche and the cupboard, and cut out a 6cm square at floor level for an electric fireplace (make provision for a string to attach to the electrical wire). Add battens to the back of the wall panel to give depth to the recesses: 10mm foamcore for the shelved niche and 5mm for the cupboard. The latter is mostly for show, since the slope of the roof does not allow it to be any deeper. The cupboard door is fixed, but if you wish you could hinge it (see page 36) and install shallow shelves inside.

3 Trim the battens to fit. At the top, to ensure a fair curve, glue in a strip of thin Bristol board: 2cm wide for the niche and 0.5cm for the cupboard. Secure this with pins driven into the underside of the foamcore batten.

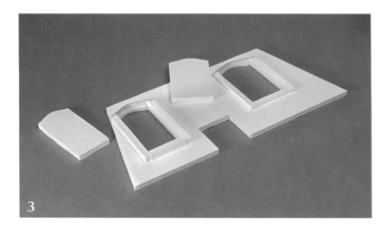

4 Glue a 13.2 x 8cm rectangle of wallpaper to a piece of Bristol board and fix this to the rear edges of the battens to form the back of the niche. Paper the sides of the niche. Prepare 2 x 6cm shelves from lime or balsa, lengths of dado moulding and a resin swag; mouldings and swags must be mitred and adjusted to fit. Paint these cream.

5 For the cupboard door, cut a frame from 3mm limewood as shown. Cut the straight lines with a utility knife; for the curves, score with the knife and then cut out with a fretsaw. Cut two lengths of 10.3 and one of 6.9cm from 5mm dado moulding. Cut the resin swag as before. Mitre the corners and glue these pieces to the frame. Paint with gesso, then finish in cream.

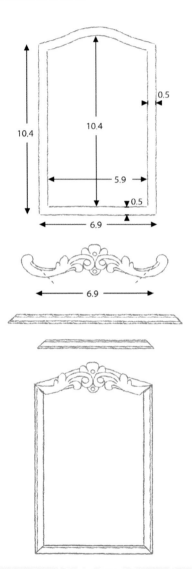

Tip

The cupboard door can be made from 1mm Bristol board: in this case, cut three identical frames (cut the curves with scissors) and glue them one on top of the other.

6 To simulate wire mesh over the door, cut a piece of tulle slightly larger than the left-hand side aperture. Paint it silver on both sides. Glue to the reverse side. Form pleats in a piece of cotton fabric (see the curtain on page 155) to cover the aperture, glue to the reverse side with the pleats running vertically, and pattern facing out. Add a lock. Apply glue to the top, bottom and left-hand edges of the wall panel and fix in place.

7 Cut a wall template from thin Bristol board. The notch in the top right corner is for a 5 x 10mm finishing batten which will be added later (see Note on page 16).

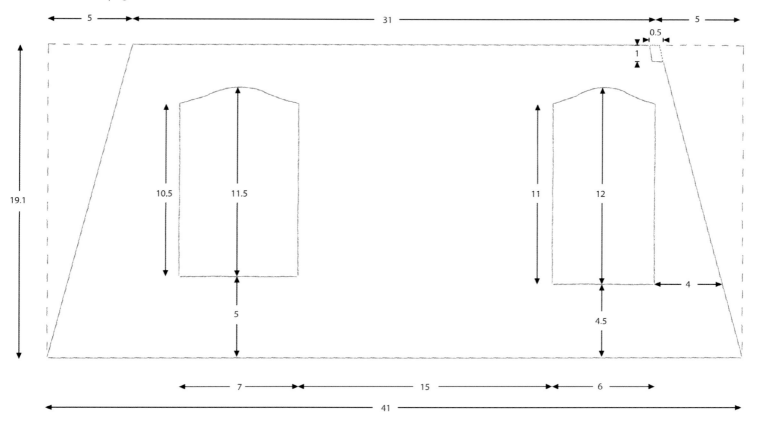

8 Cut out a mirror 7 x 8cm.

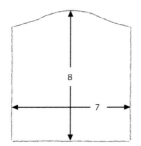

9 Cut out the mouldings etc. in the order shown (see table at right and diagram overleaf). Glue the mirror between strips no. 6 (7cm apart), using wood glue. Fix the mouldings and swag to it with contact adhesive. Apply gesso, then paint cream, protecting the mirror with masking tape. Glue on the cupboard door. Glue the template in position before adding strip 11 and the fireplace.

Tip

To make mouldings 3 and 3a, glue a 5mm moulding to a 2 x 10mm strip of limewood.

- 1: 2 x 10mm limewood strip, 30.3cm long
- 2: 13mm skirting, 17.5cm long
- 2a: 13mm skirting, 13.5cm long
- 3: Dado moulding 1 x 17cm, 3.5cm from floor
- 3a: Dado moulding 1 x 12.5cm, 3.5cm from floor
- 4: 2 x 10mm limewood strip, 2.2cm long
- 5: 2 x 10mm strip, 13.5cm long
- 6: 2 x 10mm strip, 9.5cm long
- 7: 5mm dado moulding, 7cm long
- 8: 5mm dado moulding, 7cm long
- 8a: 5mm dado moulding, cut to fit and mitred at corners
- 9: 5mm dado moulding, 6cm wide
- 9a: 5mm dado moulding, 12cm long, cut to fit and mitred at corners
- 10: Resin swag cut to 8cm (remove shell at top)
- 10a: Resin swag cut to 6cm
- 11: 0.5 x 13cm strip, cut to fit

FINISHING THE CEILING

1 Before fixing the ceiling, prepare for the electrical installation for the two rooms on this floor. In the attic bedroom, drill two holes as shown: one for the wire to the light fitting, the other to bring the wire down to the basement. For the light in the nursery, drill a hole 15cm from the near edge. Cut a 0.5 x 1cm notch at the far end, 1cm from the left-hand side, to convey the wire into the groove already prepared (see 'Cutting and assembling the roof', page 24, step 2). Glue the Bristol-board ceiling in place, passing the string for the light fitting through the hole.

2 Cut beams 1cm wide from 10mm balsa. Finish them in the same way as those in the kitchen. Angle one end of each beam to fit the slope of the roof; trim the other end off straight. Paint the beams matt white and glue them on as shown. Finish with filler as usual.

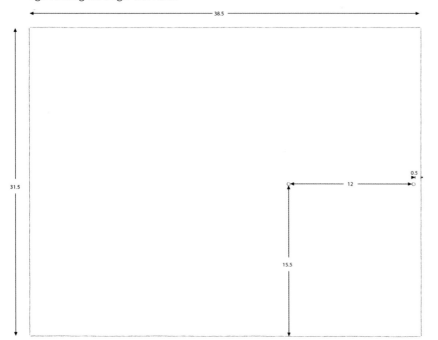

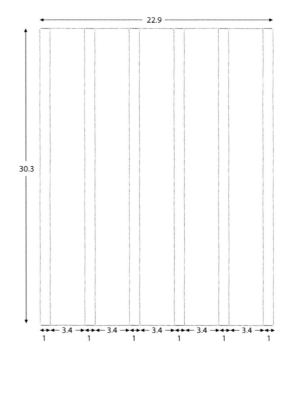

3 Pass the wire for the light fitting through the hole in the ceiling, attach it to the string already in place and pull until the light fitting is tight against the ceiling and the wire appears in the basement.

CEILING

Pass the string which is already in place through the opening in the ceiling. Cover the groove with masking tape (see page 11). The beams will be added later.

FLOOR

1 Cut a template from squared paper, 18.5 x 40.5cm. Cut out the stair opening as shown. Cover with planks cut to irregular lengths, passing beyond the edges of the template. Place under weights. Trim off the overhanging ends and cut the opening for the stairs. Paint the floor white, including all visible edges.

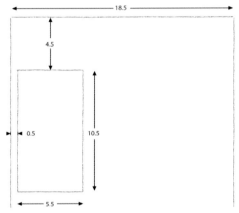

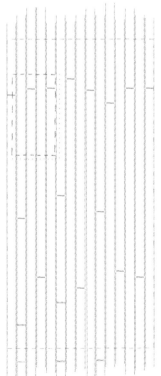

Note

The floor can be finished in various ways. For a worn effect, sand gently in the areas that get most use, apply patina 1 (page 188) and wipe off, then distress the surface by polishing with 000 steel wool.

2 To facilitate fitting the floor, cut along the dotted line. This is necessary because the handrail and safety railing are already in place (though not yet glued), and the topmost banister will be in the way. Glue the template to the floor.

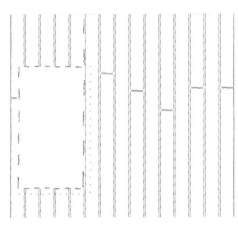

3 On the threshold between the two rooms, fill the gap between the plank floor and the parquet with a 1 x 5mm limewood strip, 6cm long, finished to match the nursery floor.

4 Superglue the banisters to the floor 0.5mm from the edge.

Tip

To apply glue to the bottoms of the banisters, put a drop of superglue on the end of a strip of wood held flat. Hold the drop of glue up to each banister in turn so that the end of the wire is dipped in the glue. Press for a few seconds to ensure that the banisters adhere to the floor.

You will need

GENERAL
- Utility knife
- 3mm gimlet
- Wood glue
- Superglue (cyanoacrylate)
- Fine glasspaper
- 000 steel wool
- Paper towel
- Paintbrushes
- Gesso
- Filler

WALLS
- Thin Bristol board
- 2 x 13mm skirting
- Satin-finish acrylic paint: soft pink

CEILING
- 8mm balsa sheet
- Matt acrylic paint: white

FLOOR
- Squared paper
- 2 x 10mm limewood strip
- Liquid wax polish
- Satin-finish acrylic paint: white

Far wall

1 Insert the window into the dormer. Cut pieces of 1mm Bristol board as shown. Paint with gesso, then paint pink before gluing into the window reveal. These pieces keep the window in place.

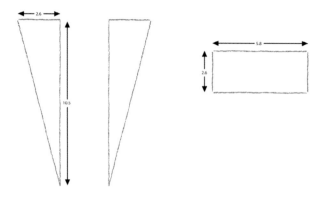

2 Cut the wall template from thin Bristol board. Angle the left-hand end to match the slope of the roof, and cut out the window opening. Since this wall slopes, access is restricted by the narrowness of the room and the presence of the safety railing. For this reason, the template is cut into three sections which are installed one after the other.

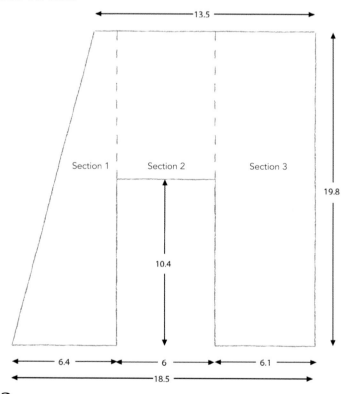

3 Draw a pencil line 5cm up from the bottom edge of the template; this is the height of the dado. On each of the three sections, assemble the woodwork in the order indicated, leaving the top 10mm uncovered until step 4. Cut the lengths of skirting straight across to the dimensions given, then angle the ends to fit as described on page 8.

Section 1
- 1: 2 x 10mm limewood strip, 18.8cm long
- 2: 2 x 10mm strip, 5.4cm long, angled to fit at left-hand end
- 3: 2 x 5mm strip, 18.5cm long, angled to fit at both ends
- 4: 2 x 10mm strip, 3.6cm long, angled to fit at left-hand end
- 5: 13mm skirting, 5.9cm long
- 6: 13mm skirting, 4cm long
- 5a, 6a, 7, 8, 9: 13mm skirting, cut to fit
- 10: 1mm Bristol board, cut as shown in the small drawing
Sand the wood panelling before fitting the dado rail (11).
- 11: 5mm dado rail, 4.5cm long, angled to fit at left-hand end

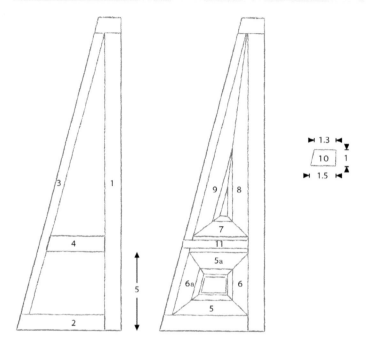

Section 2
- 12: 2 x 10mm strip, 6cm long
- 13: 13mm skirting, 6cm long

SECTION 3

- 14: 2 x 10mm limewood strip, 5.1cm long
- 15: 2 x 10mm strip, 18.8cm long
- 16: 2 x 10mm strip, 17.8cm long
- 17: 13mm skirting, 4.1cm long
- 17a: 13mm skirting, 4.1 cm long
- 18: 13mm skirting, 4cm long
- 18a: 13mm skirting, 4cm long
- 19: 13mm skirting, 4.1cm long
- 19a: 13mm skirting, 4.1cm long
- 20: 13mm skirting, 12.7cm long
- 20a: 13mm skirting, 12.7cm long
- 21: 1mm Bristol board, 1 x 0.9cm
- 22: 1mm Bristol board, 1 x 9.7cm

Sand the wood panelling before fitting the dado rail (23).

- 23: 5mm dado rail, 5.1cm long

4 Coat with gesso, then paint pink. Glue the templates to the wall. Press down section 2 with a strip of wood. Glue on a 2 x 10mm limewood strip, 14cm long (24). Apply filler as usual.

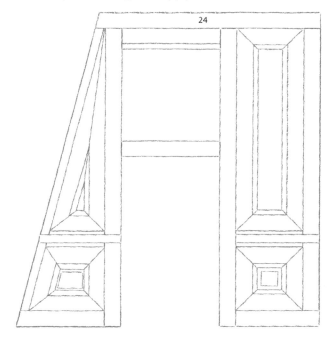

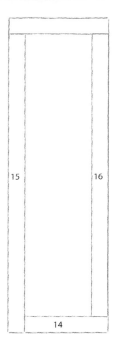

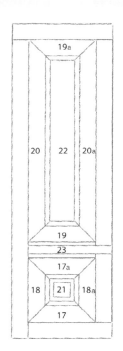

LEFT-HAND WALL

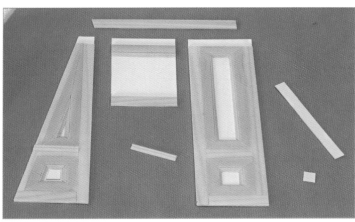

1 Cut a wall template from thin Bristol board. Cut a notch in the top left-hand corner to accommodate the 5 x 10mm finishing batten which will be installed below the ceiling.

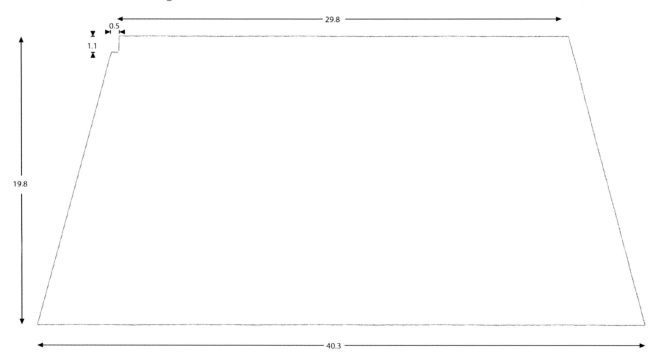

2 Trace a line on the template 5cm up from the bottom, then attach the panelling members in the order shown.

- 1: 2 x 10mm limewood strip, 40.3cm long, angled to fit at each end
- 2: 2 x 10mm limewood strip, 19.7cm long, angled to fit at each end

Now turn over the template and recut the notch from the back, following the cutout in the Bristol board.
- 3: 2 x 10mm limewood strip, 28.7cm long, angled each end
- 4: 2 x 10mm limewood strip, 35.7cm long, angled each end
- 5: 2 x 10mm limewood strip, 4cm long
- 6: 2 x 10mm limewood strip, 13.7cm long

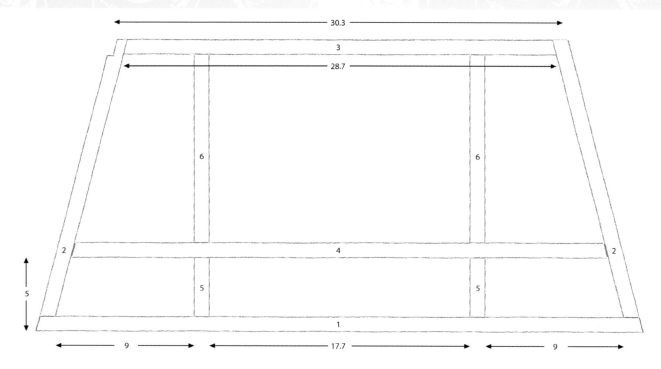

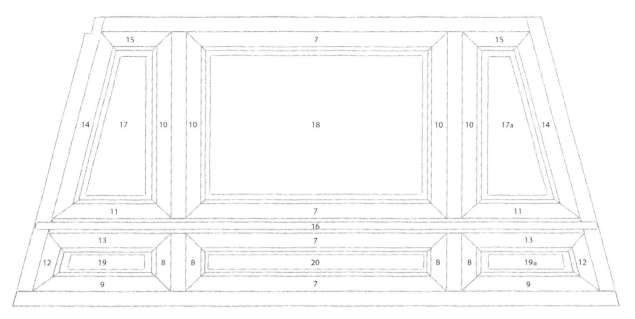

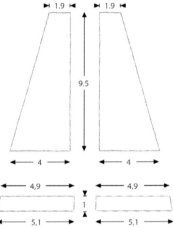

3 Coat with gesso, then paint pink. Glue the template to the wall. Finish with filler as usual.

RIGHT-HAND WALL

- 7: 13mm skirting, 17.7cm long, mitred at both ends
- 8: 13mm skirting, 4cm long, mitred at both ends
- 9: 13mm skirting, 9cm long; one end mitred to meet piece 8, other end angled to meet piece 12
- 10: 13mm skirting, 12.7cm long, mitred at both ends
- 11: 13mm skirting, 7.6cm long; one end mitred to meet piece 10, other end angled to meet piece 14
- 12: 13mm skirting, 4.1cm long, angled to fit at both ends to meet pieces 9 and 13
- 13: 13mm skirting, 7.9cm long; one end mitred to fit piece 8, other end angled to fit piece 12
- 14: 13mm skirting, 13.1cm long, angled at both ends to fit pieces 11 and 15
- 15: 13mm skirting, 4.6cm long; one end mitred to fit piece 10, other end angled to fit piece 14

Sand the woodwork before attaching the dado moulding (16).

- 16: 5mm dado moulding, 37.5cm long, angled at both ends to match the slope of the wall
- 17 and 17a: 1mm Bristol board, cut as shown in the smaller drawing
- 18: 1mm Bristol board, 9.5 x 14.3cm
- 19 and 19a: 1mm Bristol board, cut as shown in the smaller drawing
- 20: 1mm Bristol board, 1 x 14.3cm

1 Cut the wall template from thin Bristol board.

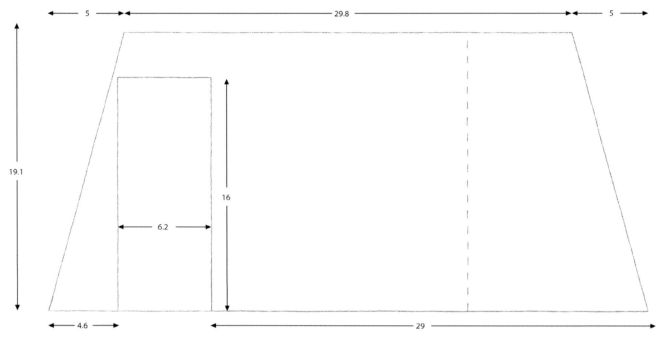

2 Draw a pencil line 5cm up from the base of the template. Apply the pieces in the following order.

- 1: 2 x 10mm limewood strip, 28cm long, angled at right end
- 1a: 2 x 10mm limewood strip, 4.2cm long, angled at left end
- 2: 2 x 10mm limewood strip, 18.1cm long
- 2a: 2 x 10mm limewood strip, 18.9cm long, angled both ends

- 3: 2 x 10mm limewood strip, 29.2cm long, angled both ends
- 4: 2 x 10mm limewood strip, 25.5cm long, angled at right end
- 5: 2 x 10mm limewood strip, 4cm long
- 6: 2 x 10mm limewood strip, 12cm long

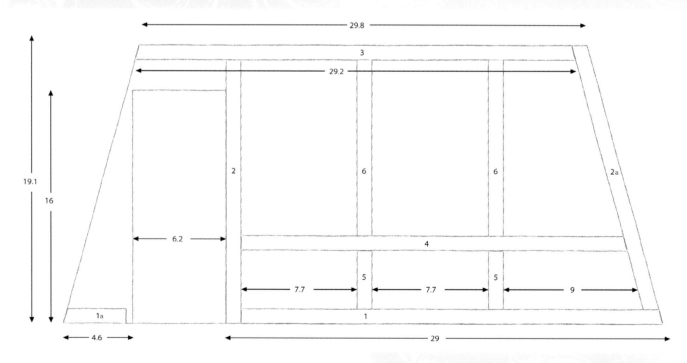

- 7: 13mm skirting, 7.7cm long, mitred at both ends
- 8: 13mm skirting, 4cm long, mitred at both ends
- 9: 13mm skirting, 9cm long, mitred at left to match piece 8, angled at right to match piece 12

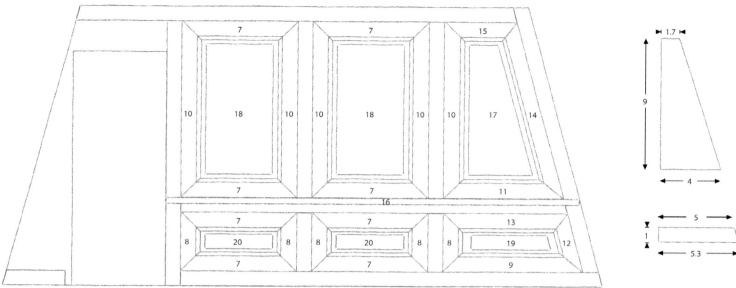

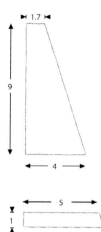

- 10: 13mm skirting, 12cm long, mitred at both ends
- 11: 13mm skirting, 7.6cm long, mitred at left to match piece 10, angled at right to match piece 14
- 12: 13mm skirting, 4.1cm long, angled to fit at both ends
- 13: 13mm skirting, 7.8cm long, mitred at left to match piece 8, angled at right to match piece 12
- 14: 13mm skirting, 12.4cm long, angled to fit at both ends
- 15: 13mm skirting, 4.3cm long, mitred at left to fit piece 10, angled at right to fit piece 14

Before attaching the dado moulding (16), sand the woodwork with fine glasspaper.

- 16: 5mm dado rail, 26.5cm long, angled to fit at right
- 17: 1mm Bristol board, cut as shown in the smaller drawing
- 18: 1mm Bristol board, 9 x 4.5cm
- 19: 1mm Bristol board, cut as shown in the smaller drawing
- 20: 1mm Bristol board, 1 x 4.5cm

3 Coat with gesso, then paint pink. Glue the template to the wall. Finish with filler as usual.

Once all the walls have been panelled, apply patina 1 (page 188).

CEILING

1 Cut six beams 1 x 13cm from 8mm balsa. Angle the left-hand end of each beam to match the slope of the wall.

Tip

To angle the end of the beam, offer the wood against the forward slope of the roof. Holding against the flat of the ceiling, mark the angle in pencil. Cut along this pencil line.

2 Paint the beams matt white. Glue the first beam 1cm in from the near edge of the ceiling, then space the others equally.

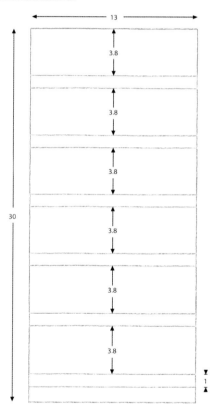

Tip

To keep the beams perfectly parallel, cut a strip of 1mm Bristol board the length of a beam and as wide as the space desired. Glue the first beam. Position the strip of Bristol board alongside this one and use it as a ruler to trace a guideline, then glue the second beam, and so on.

3 Slip the wire for the light fitting into the hole in the ceiling, attach the wire to the waiting string, then pull until the light fitting is snug against the ceiling and the wire comes through to the basement.

BEDROOMS

BELOW: UPSTAIRS AT THE VETERINARY CLINIC. *The vet's bed is made from cocktail sticks and skewers. The barber's armchair is copied from an original which I hunted down second-hand.*

OPPOSITE PAGE: *The fireplace is made of wood and painted in imitation marble.*

ABOVE:
FAMILY HOUSE.
A reproduction
of George Sand's
bedroom at the
Château de Nohant.
The fabric of the bed
canopy has been
omitted, as it would
look too coarse when
reduced to 1/12 scale.
The silk panels on
the wall are painted
freehand.

LEFT: BASTIDE. The
simple Provençal
bed, or litoche, was
traditionally crowned
with a canopy,
nowadays replaced
by a mosquito net.

*OPPOSITE PAGE: A SECRET
ROOM.* This is George
Sand's boudoir-cum-
writing-room.

LEFT AND OPPOSITE PAGE:
FLORIST'S HOUSE.
The bedroom is
decorated with
rose motifs.

LEFT: A HOUSE IN THE
COUNTRY. The petit-point
carpet is a reproduction
of an original from
the prestigious
Savonnerie carpet
works, established in
the reign of Louis XIII.

ABOVE: BASTIDE. This feminine room brings together costume and accessories typical of the ladies of Arles in Provence.

LEFT: FAMILY HOUSE. The delicate shades of this guest bedroom evoke the end of the 18th century.

OPPOSIITE PAGE, TOP: A HOUSE IN THE COUNTRY. Net curtains, old lace, wooden boarding on the walls and painted floorboards create a delightful effect.

OPPOSITE PAGE, BOTTOM: CHALET. The flaking finish on the walls suggests limewash. The patchwork quilt is made of hexagonal panels sewn together with blind stitches.

FURNITURE AND FITTINGS

You will need

- 1mm Bristol board
- Thin Bristol board
- 3mm foam
- 2 medium turned spindles (front legs)
- 2 thicker turned spindles (back legs)
- 6 thin turned spindles (side stretchers and arm supports)
- 3 cocktail sticks
- 2 wooden knobs
- Crochet cotton, ecru
- Gesso
- Satin-finish acrylic paints:
    off-white
    brown (optional)
- Paintbrushes
- Compass point
- Scissors
- Wool needle
- Quick-setting wood glue
- Fine glasspaper
- 000 steel wool

PROVENÇAL ARMCHAIR

1 Cut three of each piece shown below from 1mm Bristol board. Glue together the three copies of each shape to give an overall thickness of 3mm.

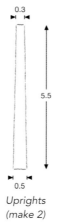

Uprights
(make 2)

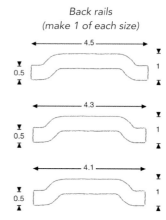

Back rails
(make 1 of each size)

Arms (make 2)

2 Mark guidelines on the front face of each upright to show where the curved back rails go. Prepare two front legs (a), two back legs (b) and four side stretchers (c).

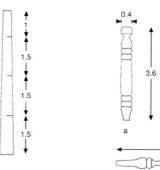

3 For each arm support, cut down a thin turned spindle to a length of 2cm (c'). Cut two pieces of cocktail stick 4.5cm long (d), and another of 4cm (d').

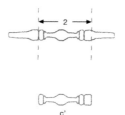

c'

4 Assemble as shown.

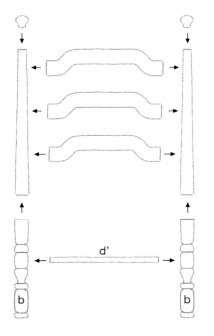

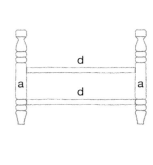

5 Join the back and front assemblies together with two side stretchers (c) on each side. Glue the two arm supports (c') to the arms. Coat all the parts with gesso, then paint brown if you want an aged effect. Paint over this with off-white. Sand the edges to simulate wear, then apply patina 1 (page 188).

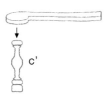

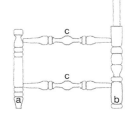

6 Simplified method for rush seating: cut out the shape to be covered from thin Bristol board and draw two diagonals. Using a compass point dipped in wood glue, make a small hole every 3mm or so along both diagonals, beginning at the centre. Cut a piece of 3mm foam to the same shape. Fix this on top of the Bristol board with a spot of wood glue at each corner.

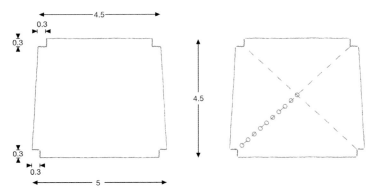

7 Thread the needle with a length of cotton folded double. The seat is woven one quarter at a time, but beginning and ending halfway through one of the quarters. To start, pass the needle up through the central hole and then through the foam.

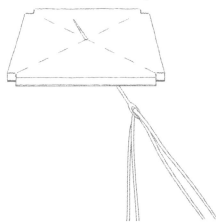

8 Pass the needle over the edge of the seat (keeping the thread exactly parallel to the front edge of the seat), then slip it through the loop and pull the loop tight against the Bristol board. This method avoids starting the weaving with a knot.

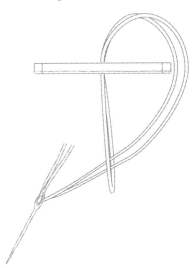

9 Insert the needle into the next hole, still from beneath, and continue in this way, ensuring that the threads remain parallel. When you get to the corner, continue by coming back along the same diagonal to form the second quarter of the seat. Put a drop of glue under the threads at each of the notches.

10 Glue the seat to the chair frame by the notches at the corners. Finally, glue on the arms.

You will need

- 1mm Bristol board
- Mirrored acetate
- 2mm gilt paper frieze
- 2mm twisted braid
- Gesso
- Modelmaking paint, gold
- Paintbrushes
- Utility knife
- Scissors
- Quick-setting wood glue
- Solvent-free contact adhesive

MIRRORS

SMALL VERSION

1 Cut two rectangles 4.5 x 6cm from 1mm Bristol board, and a piece of mirrored acetate the same size. Round off the upper corners. Cut out the centre of one of the pieces of Bristol board to leave a frame 0.3cm wide.

2 Coat the pieces of Bristol board with gesso, then gold paint. Glue the frieze of gilt paper to the front of the frame.

3 Put a drop of wood glue on the back of the mirror at each corner. Glue the mirror to the backing piece. Fix the frame to the front of the mirror with contact adhesive. Weight until dry. Retouch the edges.

Note

The small mirror is sandwiched between two layers of Bristol board; the large one is cut to fit inside the opening of the frame.

LARGE VERSION

1 Cut two rectangles 6 x 8cm and a strip 0.5 x 6cm from 1mm Bristol board. Cut a piece of mirror 5 x 7cm. Round off the upper corners. Cut out one of the rectangles of Bristol board to make a frame 0.5cm wide.

2 Glue the frame to the backing piece. Glue the 0.5mm strip along the bottom edge. Weight down for a few minutes, then glue on the braid. Coat with gesso, then paint gold. Glue the mirror into the opening.

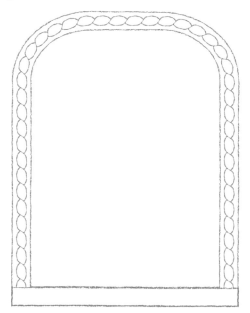

You will need

- 1mm Bristol board
- Thin Bristol board
- 5mm foamcore
- 10mm foamcore
- 2 wooden banisters
- 2 buttons with shanks, or round wooden doorknobs
- Cotton fabric, A4 size
- Gold braid, or DMC embroidery thread in 2 strands
- 8 gilt-paper rosettes
- Gesso
- Modelmaking paint, gold
- Paintbrushes
- Scissors
- Quick-setting wood glue

LOUIS XVI SOFA

1 Cut three of each shape from 1mm Bristol board. Glue the three layers together to make an overall thickness of 3mm.

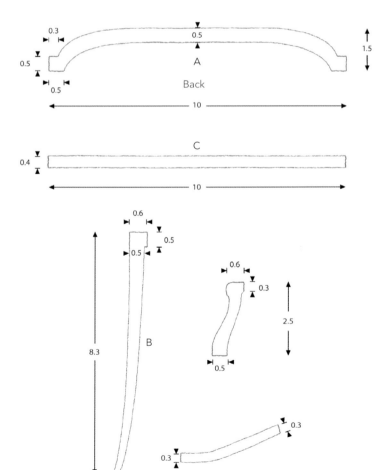

Note

The sofa can also be made from wood 3mm thick, by cutting out the parts with a fretsaw.

2 Cut the two front legs, 3.1cm long, from wooden banisters. Whittle them down with the utility knife. Cut a tiny strip, 1 x 1mm and 1cm long, from the edge of the 1mm Bristol board. Glue this around the foot, 2mm from the lower end.

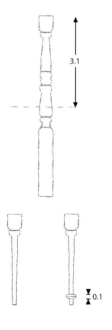

3 Cut three seat shapes (D) from 1mm Bristol board and glue them together to make a single thickness of 3mm.

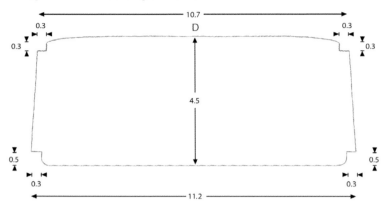

4 Glue the front legs into their notches.

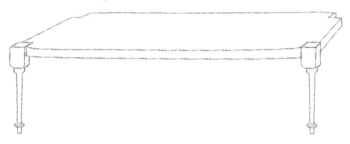

5 Assemble the back of the sofa frame as shown. Glue the seat level (D) between the uprights (B), ensuring that the back legs equal the height of the front ones.

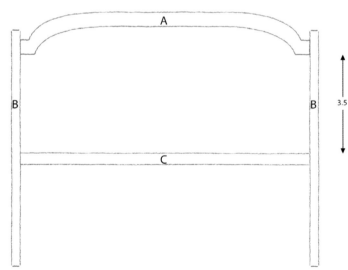

6 Assemble the armrests, trimming the ends as necessary to match the slope of the uprights. Glue in place and leave to dry thoroughly. Glue a button, shank uppermost, to the top of each upright.

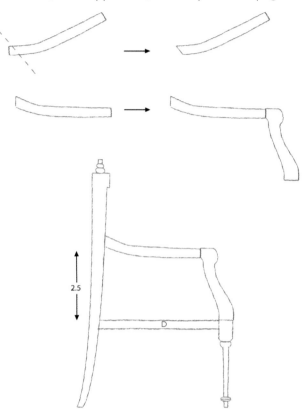

7 Protect the whole assembly with a coat of gesso (since the gold modelling paint is solvent-based, there is a risk of dissolving the glue). Paint gold, and wipe off in places to bring out some white highlights. The frame is now ready to receive the upholstered armrests, seat and back.

Note

To create hand-embroidered tapestry, you will need a miniature canvas such as silk gauze or similar, embroidery cotton and a suitable motif. Or you can simply print the motif onto fine ecru or white cotton fabric using an office printer. If the fabric is too flimsy to go through your printer, cut it down a little so that the edges can be taped to an A4 sheet of paper. Set the print quality to maximum and select 'special papers'.

8 Cut out the seat shape in 10mm foamcore, and cut the back upholstery from 5mm foamcore. Adjust these pieces to fit as necessary. Remove the layer of paper from the top of the seat piece and round over the front and side edges using scissors. Round all four edges of the back in the same way. Cover both pieces with fabric and glue in place.

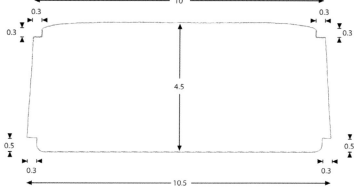

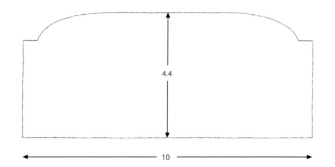

9 Retrieve the paper film that you removed from the foamcore used for the back. Cover this with plain-coloured fabric and glue to the reverse of the sofa back.

10 For each armrest, cut a piece of fabric 1.5cm square. Fold back 0.5cm along two opposite sides. The finished armrest pad measures 0.5 x 1.5cm. Round the ends.

11 Glue braid trim around the upholstered parts (to make your own braid from embroidery thread, see page 150, step 11). For the characteristically 18th-century bow at the top, cut a strip of thin Bristol board 0.1 x 10cm. Pleat this as closely as possible. Apply wood glue to the middle 2cm of the top edge of the sofa back. Lay the pleated ribbon flat on the glued edge. Form the bow at the top by making three loops one beside the other, leaving about 1cm of ribbon on either side. Paint gold.

12 Attach the gilt-paper rosettes to the frame.

You will need

- The construction method and the materials required are the same as for the Louis XVI sofa (see pages 145–147).

LOUIS XVI BERGÈRE

1 Cut three of each shape from 1mm Bristol board. Glue the three layers together to make an overall thickness of 3mm.

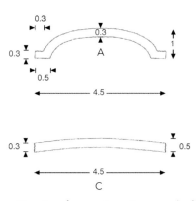

Drawings for step 1 continue overleaf.

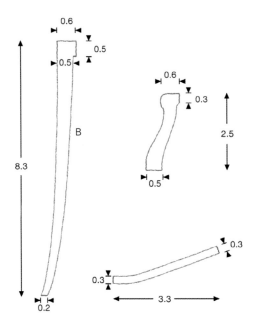

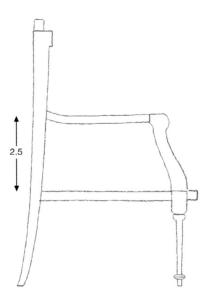

2 Construct legs and seat, assemble, add armrests and paint, as for the sofa.

3 Make the seat upholstery from 10mm foamcore and that for the back from 5mm, as for the sofa. Finish as before.

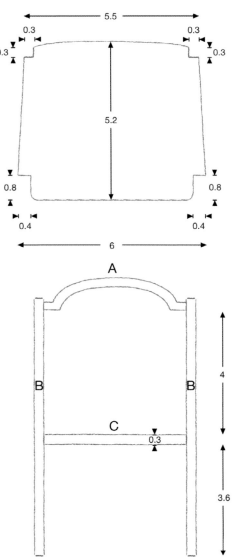

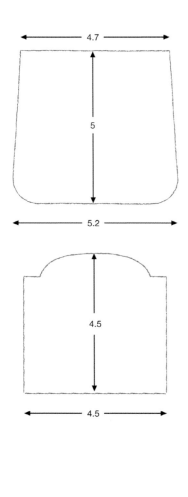

LOUIS XV CABRIOLET

1 Cut out three of each part from 1mm Bristol board. Cut out the centre of the back with the fretsaw and keep the offcut. Laminate the three copies of each part to make a total thickness of 3mm.

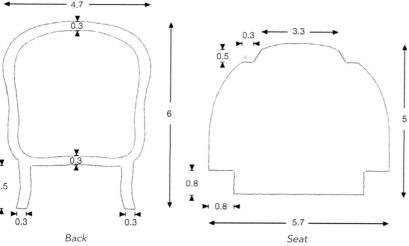

Back

Seat

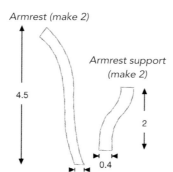

Armrest (make 2)

Armrest support (make 2)

Apron

You will need

- 1mm Bristol board
- Thin Bristol board
- 5mm foamcore
- 10mm foamcore
- 4 wooden cabriole legs, 3.5cm long
- Cotton fabric, A4 size
- DMC cotton embroidery thread, 2 strands
- Paper rosettes and leaves
- Gesso
- Modelmaking paint, gold
- Paintbrushes
- Scissors
- Fretsaw
- Quick-setting wood glue

2 Glue the back to the seat. Glue the apron to the front edge of the seat. Glue on the relief decorations (two rosettes and two leaves).

3 Glue on the wooden legs: the rear ones are placed over the notches that are filled by the back uprights, while the front ones fit into the notches at the front.

4 Assemble the armrests and their supports. Curve the front end of the armrest. Glue on the support and then glue the whole assembly in place. If necessary, adjust the angle where the armrest meets the outside edge of the back.

5 When the glue is completely dry, coat with gesso, which will protect the glue joints from the solvent-based modelmaking paint. When this undercoat is quite dry, apply the gold paint, wiping it off in places to reveal patches of white to give an effect of natural wear. The frame is now ready to receive the arm pads, seat and back upholstered in printed cotton or silk (see pages 146–7).

6 Retrieve the offcut from the back and draw round this onto 5mm foamcore. Cut out the foamcore and peel off the paper layer from the front surface. Round over the edges of the outline.

7 Transfer the outline of the seat onto 10mm foamcore.

8 Cover both pieces of foamcore with printed fabric, then glue them in place.

9 For each armrest, cut a rectangle of fabric 1.5 x 2cm. Turn back 0.5cm along each side. The finished piece measures 0.5 x 2cm. Round over the ends.

10 Retrieve the paper layer that you removed from the foamcore for the back. Cover this with fabric in a solid colour and glue to the reverse side of the backrest.

11 Make a finishing braid as follows: take a 1m length of embroidery cotton. Fold it in two, twist it, then fold in two again; it will twine around itself to form a narrow braid. It will keep together better if you glue it lightly along its whole length. Fix it around the edges of the seat, back and arm pads.

You will need

- 1mm Bristol board
- Thin Bristol board
- 3mm foam
- Scissors
- Utility knife
- Quick-setting wood glue
- Contact adhesive
- 2 wooden banisters
- 2 dressmaking pins
- 8 gilt-paper rosettes
- Fine cotton canvas or printed cotton fabric
- DMC embroidery cotton, 2 strands
- Gold braid

LOUIS XVI SIDE CHAIR

1 Cut out three of each part shown below from 1mm Bristol board. Assemble the three layers to give a total thickness of 3mm.

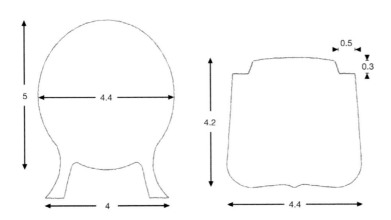

2 Do the same with the back legs (cut out six parts to make the two legs).

3 For the front legs, cut the two banisters to a length of 3.5cm. Whittle them down with the utility knife. Cut a tiny strip of 1mm Bristol board (see page 145, step 2) and glue around the foot, 2mm from the end.

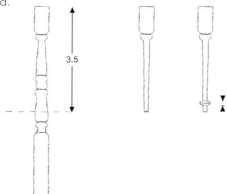

4 Glue the back to the seat; the back must fit into the notches without protruding below the seat. Glue on the back legs with the concave side facing the rear. Glue the front legs as described for the large screen (page 152, step 5).

5 Coat with gesso, then paint gold, as for the Louis XV cabriolet.

6 Transfer the shape of the seat onto thin Bristol board (see step 1). Cut out the same shape in foam.

7 Lay the foam over the Bristol board. Place both on the fabric, so that the foam is in contact with the reverse of the fabric. Cut out the fabric, leaving a margin of 1cm all round. Fold back the surplus fabric and glue it to the back of the Bristol board. Glue the seat cushion to the seat.

8 For the back, transfer the shape below onto thin Bristol board, then proceed as for the seat. Cut an identical shape in thin Bristol board, cover with plain-coloured fabric and glue to the reverse of the chair back.

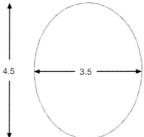

9 Use contact adhesive to glue a narrow gold braid (or gold elastic as used for the large screen) all round the oval of the chair back, 1mm from the edge. Do the same around the edge of the seat. Apply a finishing braid made from embroidery thread (see Louis XV cabriolet, step 11) around the seat cushion and the back.

10 Glue paper rosettes to the outside surfaces of the square part of the front legs.

You will need

- 1mm Bristol board
- Thin Bristol board
- Copier paper
- Mirrored acetate
- 4 wooden banisters
- Gold elastic
- 20 gilt-paper rosettes
- Gesso
- Modelmaking paint, gold
- Paintbrushes
- Utility knife
- Scissors
- Dressmaking pins
- Masking tape
- Wood glue
- Transparent, solvent-free contact adhesive

LARGE FOLDING SCREEN

1 Cut out six rectangles 13 x 4cm from 1mm Bristol board, and three identical pieces of mirrored acetate.

2 Cut the upper part to shape, then cut openings in three of the pieces of Bristol board, as shown.

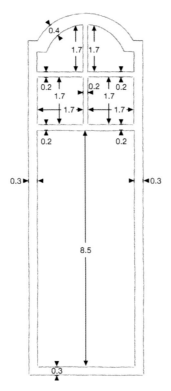

3 Coat with gesso then paint gold, including all the edges. Fold four srips of masking tape, then fix them with wood glue to the three solid panels as shown, taking care to keep the panels parallel.

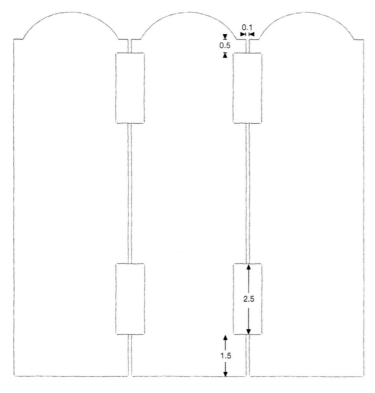

4 Fix the mirrors to the panels with wood glue. The tape, sandwiched between the Bristol board and the mirror, forms the hinges. Glue one of the cut-out pieces of Bristol board over each mirror.

5 For the feet, cut four banisters to a length of 1.8cm. Whittle them down with the utility knife, then paint. To reinforce the joints, insert a pin into the top of each foot. Cut the pin so that it projects 0.3cm. Remove the pin, dip the cut end into glue and plant it back in the hole. Apply glue to the point of the pin, then push this into the base of the screen. Paint the feet to match the frame.

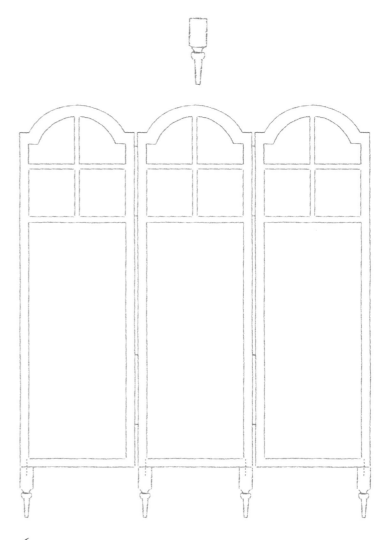

6 Glue on the gold elastic trim; add the rosettes, and make pleated bows with two loops each (see page 147, step 11). This time the strips for the bows are 8cm long. Glue printed paper to the lower panels (covering the acetate) with a thin coat of wood glue.

PELMET AND CURTAINS

You will need

- 1mm Bristol board
- Thin Bristol board
- Silk paper (or copier paper)
- Picture-frame moulding
- 5 x 10mm limewood strip
- Floral printed fabric, 25 x 45cm
- Needle and thread
- Festooned or fringed braid
- Narrow ribbon
- Gilt-paper friezes and flowers
- Gesso
- Modelmaking paint, gold
- Satin-finish acrylic paint, pearl-grey (equal parts cream and light grey)
- Paintbrushes
- Utility knife
- Scissors
- Small mitre box
- Razor saw
- Wood glue
- Domestic iron
- Pleating tool, large (see Note, page 155)
- Starch

PELMET

1 Cut a rectangle 2 x 11cm from 1mm Bristol board. Score with the utility knife 0.5cm in from each end, and fold. Coat with gesso (including the score marks), then paint pearl-grey.

2 Cut a hollow oval from 1mm Bristol board as shown. Coat with gesso, then paint gold.

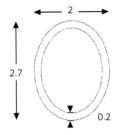

3 Glue the oval frame to some printed fabric, keeping the motif centred in the frame. Cut off the excess fabric and glue fine Bristol board to the back. Fix the oval to the pelmet; it should overhang at the top.

4 Take a length of picture-frame moulding and paint it gold. Cut four sections, mitring the ends as shown to fit the pelmet.

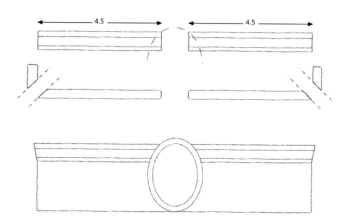

5 Cut a 10cm length of 5 x 10mm batten. Glue this inside the folded Bristol board, flush with the top of the moulding. The curtains will be attached to the underside of this batten.

View from above

6 Add the trim, including a pleated bow with two loops, made from a 10cm strip of thin Bristol board (see page 147, step 11).

CURTAINS

Note

The dimensions given for the curtains are appropriate for a ceiling height of 23cm.

1 For the fringes, cut a strip of thin ecru fabric 0.8 x 20cm. Fray the edge to a width of 0.5cm.

2 Cut paper patterns for the drapes (A, B and A'). Pin these to the fabric and cut along the edges. From the remaining fabric, cut a rectangle 18 x 20cm (C).

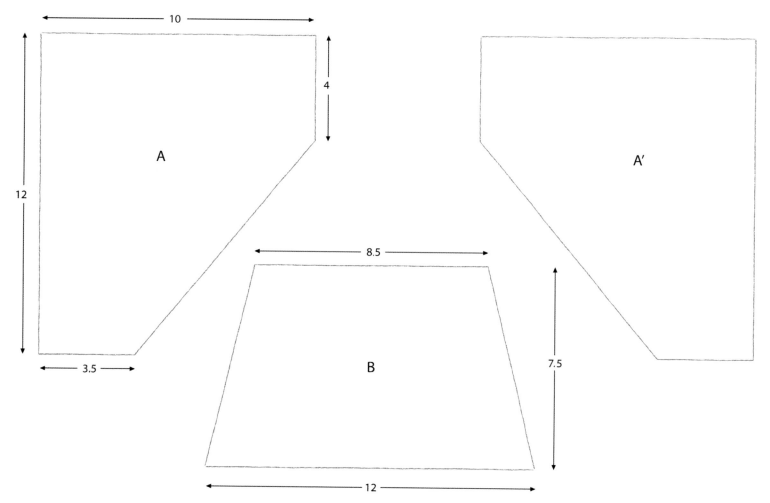

3 Glue on the fringes, then fold shapes A and A' accordion-fashion as shown at right. Iron to fix the pleats. Make the fringes hang downwards.

Note

The pleating tool is a slab of heat-resistant rubber with regular grooves in the surface. Pleating is done with a wooden stick and a plastic card, supplied with the tool. Once the fabric has been pleated, it can be left in place for ironing (with the aid of a damp cloth) to accentuate the pleats.

4 Place the fabric piece B on the pleating tool. The pleats in B should be parallel to the bottom edge. Starch the fabric. Use the wooden stick to push the edge of the fabric into the first groove. Hold it in the groove with one hand; with the other hand, smooth it down into the second groove with the aid of the card. Continue until all the pleats are formed.

5 Starch the rectangular piece C, and when dry make pleats using the pleater. Cut piece C lengthways into two rectangles of equal width (C and C'). Glue the fringes to the edges of pieces B, C and C'. The fringed edge of B runs parallel to the pleats.

6 With needle and thread, gather the two ends of piece B. Glue this piece to the underside of the 5 x 10mm batten. Adjust the gathered edges below the batten to form a rounded drape. Glue A and A' in front and C and C' behind. Use a piece of narrow ribbon as a tie back.

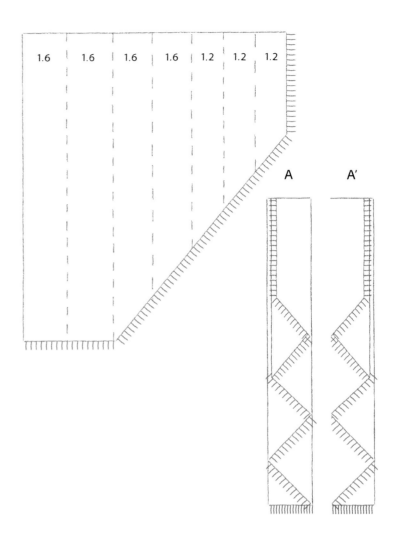

You will need

For each light fitting:
- 1mm Bristol board
- 0.5mm florists' wire.
- Sewing thread and patchwork needle
- 2 electric candles, 4.8cm, with plug
- 2 lightbulbs with filaments, 0.3cm (see step 10)
- 2 perforated sequins, 0.8cm
- Transparent glass beads (pendants):
    3 round, 0.2cm diameter
    5 oval, 0.2cm diameter, 0.9cm long
- Gesso
- Modelmaking paint, gold
- Paintbrushes
- Needle-nosed pliers
- Wire strippers or side-cutting pliers
- Tweezers
- Scissors
- Compass point
- Quick-setting wood glue
- Superglue (cyanoacrylate)

LOUIS XV WALL SCONCES FOR THE SALON

1 Cut out the shape shown from 1mm Bristol board. Use a compass point dipped in a drop of wood glue to make holes for the florists' wire. Cut three 2cm lengths of wire and shape them with the needle-nosed pliers. Dip the bottom ends in wood glue and glue them into the three upper holes, with the loops facing forward.

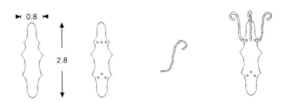

2 Cut two more 2cm lengths of wire and shape as shown. Dip the end without the loop into a drop of wood glue and fit a sequin onto the end. Leave to dry.

3 Attach the candle, plaiting the electrical wires around the florists' wire. Pass the wires through one of the holes at the bottom. On the back of the sconce, bring together the stripped ends of the wires so they can't be confused with those of the other candle when it comes to fitting the plug. Do the same with the other candle.

4 Sew the candleholders to the sconce. Slip a needle and a double length of thread into one of the holes from behind, pass it through the loop in the florists' wire, then return to the back of the sconce through the same hole. Pass the needle through the opposite hole, bring to the front, pass it through the loop of the other candleholder, return to the back and tie off with a double knot. Put a drop of wood glue where each loop of wire touches the sconce.

Take care!

Use acrylic wood glue. A solvent-based glue would damage the plastic sheathing of the electric wires and could cause a short circuit.

5 Cut and shape two 2cm lengths of florists' wire. Glue these to the convex side of the candleholders. Cut and shape a 1.5cm length and glue this into the remaining hole in the sconce, as in step 1.

 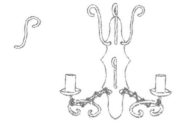

6 Strip the last 0.5cm of the electrical wire. Each candle has two wires: a and b for candle A, a' and b' for candle B. Bring together the stripped ends of aa' and bb'.

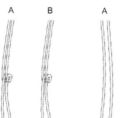 

7 Remove the metal contacts from the plug, then pass the wires through the central hole. Insert the stripped ends of aa' and bb' into the housings on either side of the central hole, then replace the contacts.

 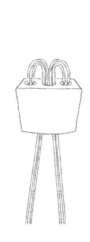 

a a' b b'

8 Apply gesso to the whole of the light fitting, except for the candles. Paint gold.

9 Dip some sewing thread into the gold paint, wipe off and leave to dry. The thread is now stiff and gold-coloured. Cut a 5cm length and knot one end. Dip the knot in a drop of wood glue. Insert the thread into one of the glass beads; the knot blocks the thread in the bead and prevents it from pulling through. Leave about 0.5cm of thread protruding from the top of the bead. Grasping the bead with tweezers, dip the end of the thread into a drop of superglue. Glue the thread to the light fitting, pressing it in place with the tip of the tweezers. Leave to dry.

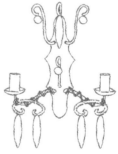

10 The bulbs have two filaments which form an electrical contact when inserted into the candles. Cut the filaments 0.3cm long and insert into the holes provided.

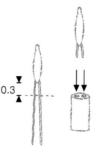

PENDANT LIGHT FOR SALON

1 Cut three pieces of florists' wire 9.5cm long (A), three pieces 2cm long (B) and three pieces 2.5cm long (C). Shape with pliers.

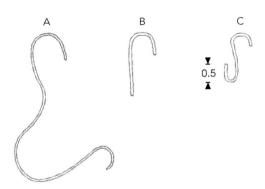

2 Next, cut two rings from 1mm Bristol board, 0.5 x 1cm and 0.5 x 0.5cm diameter.

3 Glue the three pieces C at equal distances around the larger ring, pressing the lower loop of the wire against the ring. Glue the three pieces A between them. Glue the three pieces B halfway up pieces C. Glue the tops of pieces A to the smaller ring.

4 Glue the three small bowls to the end of each piece A. Allow the glue to dry. Apply a first coat of gesso all over.

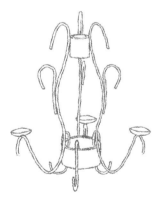

5 Pass the wires for the candles through the centre of each bowl; plait the wires below the loop and all the way along piece A as far as the small ring. Pass the rest of the wire through the ring. Tie the wires for each candle together so they cannot be confused. Fit the bulbs as before (page 156 step 10).

You will need

- 1mm Bristol board
- White 0.5mm florists' wire
- Sewing thread and patchwork needle
- 3 electric candles, 4.8mm, with plug
- 3 bulbs with filaments, 0.2cm
- 3 perforated sequins, 0.8cm diameter
- Transparent glass beads (pendants):
    3 round, 0.2cm diameter
    5 oval, 0.2cm diameter, 0.9cm long
    1 drop, 1cm long
- Gesso
- Modelmaking paint, gold
- Paintbrushes
- Needle-nosed pliers
- Wire strippers or side-cutting pliers
- Tweezers
- Scissors
- Quick-setting wood glue
- Superglue (cyanoacrylate)

6 Attach the plug as before. This time there are three pairs of wires (A, B, C). Strip the last 0.5cm of each wire.

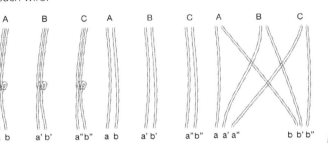

7 Proceed as for the wall fittings.

8 Apply another coat of gesso to everything except the candles. Paint gold. Add beads and pendants to the end of each curved section, as for the wall sconces. Refer to the picture on page 90.

You will need

- 1mm Bristol board
- Thin Bristol board
- Gilt-paper rosette
- Cotton fabric, A4 size
- Gesso
- Modelmaking paint, gold
- Paintbrushes
- Scissors
- Wood glue

FIRE SCREEN

1 Cut two pieces of 1mm Bristol board and one piece of fabric as shown. Coat with gesso, then paint gold.

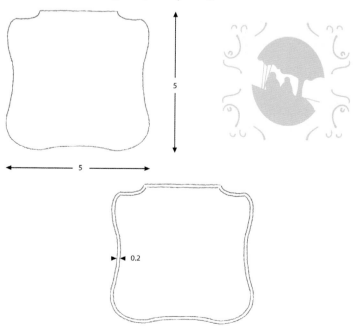

2 Glue the fabric to the backing piece and glue the frame on top.

3 For each foot, cut two identical shapes from 1mm Bristol board and glue these together. Place under weights. Coat with gesso, then paint gold.

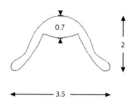

4 Cut a notch at the top.

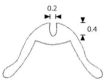

5 Glue the feet to the underside of the fire screen as shown. Add a pleated ribbon as for the large screen (page 152).

You will need

- 3mm limewood sheet
- 1mm limewood sheet
- 1mm florists' wire, white
- Copier paper
- Mirrored acetate
- Picture, 4.4cm square
- 3 cocktail sticks with turned ends
- 2mm flat braid
- Gilt-paper flowers
- Sewing thread
- Modelmaking paint, gold
- Satin-finish acrylic paint, mouse-grey
- Paintbrushes
- Utility knife
- Side-cutting pliers
- Scissors
- Quick-setting wood glue

OVERMANTEL

1 Cut a rectangle 7.5 x 10cm from 3mm lime. Cut a strip 0.5 x 7.5cm (c) from 1mm lime and glue this across the bottom of the first piece, flush with the edges. Coat both sides with gesso, then paint grey. Apply patina 1 (page 188) to both sides. Cut a strip 0.2 x 7.5cm (a) from 1mm lime, and another four pieces 0.2 x 9.3cm (b). Paint these gold and glue into place.

2 Cut 13cm of wire and form into a circle of 4.3cm diameter. There is no need to join the ends. Paint gold, then place the circle over your chosen picture. Cut out the picture so that it does not project beyond the circle. Glue the picture to the overmantel, then glue the circle on top, with the ends of the wire at the top.

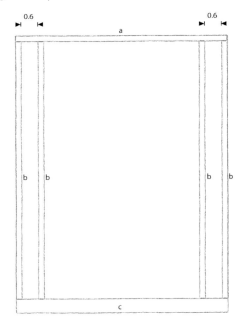

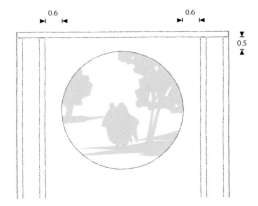

3 Cut the mirror to 3.5 x 4.5cm. Fix it with wood glue so that it rests on the crosspiece c.

4 Cut a 4cm length of cocktail stick. Cut it in two lengthwise by making a short cut at each end, then holding it down with a ruler while you run the blade along it. Cut a 2cm length of cocktail stick and treat this in the same way.

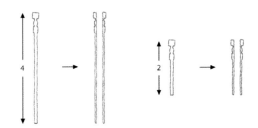

5 Cut another 4.5cm section from the unturned part of a cocktail stick and cut it in two lengthwise as before. Cut two 0.2cm discs from the turned part. Cut a rectangle 0.3 x 0.6cm from 1mm lime.

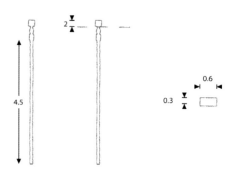

6 Paint all the parts gold and leave to dry. Glue all these trim pieces around the mirror. Cut 15cm of flat braid. Dip it in gold paint, then wipe off the surplus and leave to dry. Make it into a bow and glue it to the top of the wire circle.

7 To cut rose leaves from paper, fold the paper accordion-fashion into three thicknesses. Fold the whole thing in two, then cut a half-leaf with the scissors along the fold line.

8 Cut six 1.5cm lengths of sewing thread. Fix the leaves to the threads with wood glue.

9 Paint the six sets of leaves gold on both sides and glue them around the lower edge of the wire circle. Add the paper flowers, painted gold.

You will need

- 1, 2, 3 and 10mm limewood sheet
- Dado moulding
- Gesso
- Satin-finish acrylic paints:
    black
    English rose
    tan
    dolphin grey
    white
- Gloss acrylic varnish
- Paintbrushes
- Utility knife
- Fretsaw
- Clamps
- Quick-setting wood glue

LOUIS XVI CHIMNEYPIECE FOR THE SALON

1 Cut two identical shapes from 10mm lime. Glue them together to give a total thickness of 2cm. Clamp until dry.

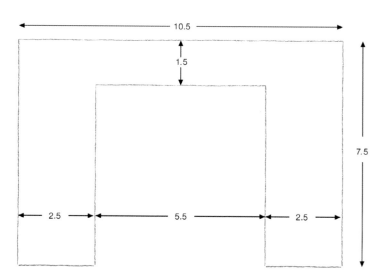

2 Cut a further piece from 1mm lime to the dimensions shown on the next page. Glue this to the previous two layers so as to form a relief around the fireplace. Clamp or weight until dry.

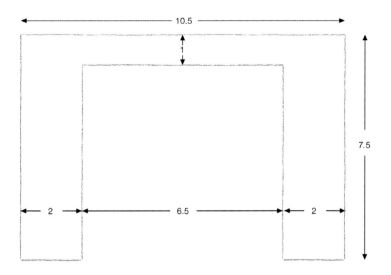

3 Cut two rectangles 2.5 x 7.5cm from 3mm lime. Glue two lengths of dado moulding 7.5cm long to each rectangle. Glue these pieces to the front of the chimneypiece, either side of the hearth.

4 Cut a rectangle 2.8 x 11cm from 2mm lime. Cut a rectangle 2.5 x 10.3cm from 10mm lime. Glue these pieces to the top of the chimneypiece, keeping their back edges flush with the back of the structure.

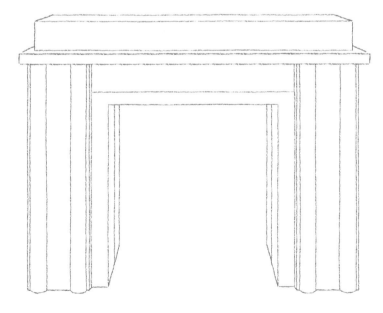

5 Cut a rectangle 3 x 11cm from 3mm lime. Glue this to the 10mm piece you have just fitted, keeping the back edge level with the back of the structure.

6 Cut four rectangles and four narrow strips of 1mm lime as shown, then glue these to the sides of the chimneypiece.

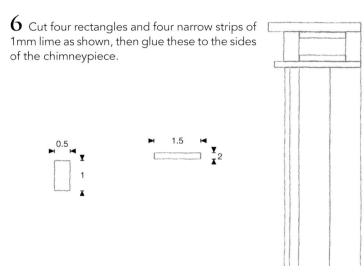

7 For the front trim, cut and glue four more pieces as shown.

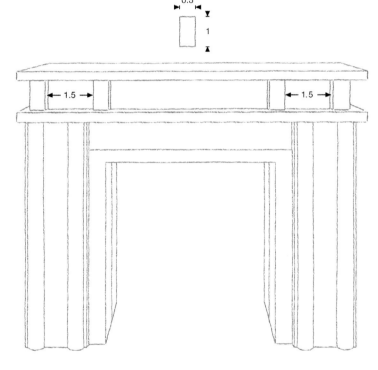

8 Cut two long and four short strips of 1mm lime and glue these to the top and bottom edges of the three rectangular panels formed in the previous step.

9 Apply a coat of gesso to the whole piece. Paint the inside of the fireplace black. Paint the outside in imitation marble (see page 188) and varnish.

LOW TABLE

1 From 3mm limewood sheet, cut two rectangles 3 x 8.5cm, two apron pieces 1.2 x 7.2cm, two aprons 1.2 x 4.7cm and a shelf 5 x 8cm. Cut out the corners of the shelf as shown.

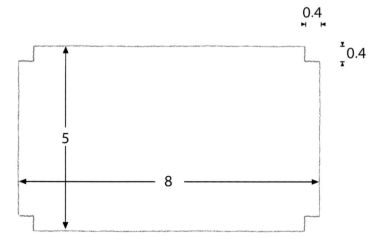

0.4

0.4

5

8

2 Cut four legs 4cm long from the 5 x 5mm batten. On two sides of each leg, make a mark 1.2cm up to indicate the position of the shelf.

3 Assemble the two sections of the table top with wood glue. Put the assembly under weights to make sure it stays properly flat. Mark the positions of the square legs on the underside of the table top. Mark two diagonals in each of these squares. Drive a pin into the centre of each cross. Glue on the legs 1mm in from the edges of the table top, reinforcing the joints with pins (see page 152, step 5).

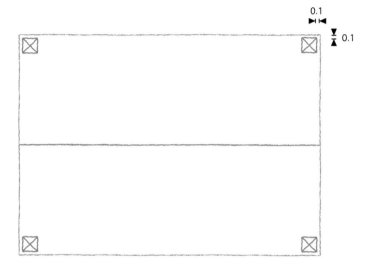

0.1

0.1

4 Glue on the aprons, level with the inside corners of the legs.

5 Apply glue to the notches in the shelf. Glue the shelf on, referring to the guides marked on the legs. Clamp until dry.

6 Apply a coat of paint to the whole table. Wipe off with a soft rag while still wet. Apply a coat of bleached oak woodstain. Wipe over with steel wool, rubbing more or less gently to achieve the desired degree of ageing.

CHILD'S BED

You will need

- 1mm Bristol board
- Thin Bristol board
- 10mm foamcore
- Florists' wire, white, 1mm and 1.5mm
- Thin wire
- Cotton fabric
- 4 small casters (optional)
- Gesso
- Satin-finish acrylic paint: off-white
- Paintbrushes
- Utility knife
- Scissors
- Side-cutting pliers
- Flat-nosed pliers
- Compass point
- Quick-setting wood glue
- Superglue (cyanoacrylate)

1 Cut a bed base 6.5 x 12cm from 1mm Bristol board. Make a small hole in each corner, about 1mm in.

2 Cut two lengths of 1.5mm wire, 21.5cm long, for the head and foot of the cot. Shape these as shown.

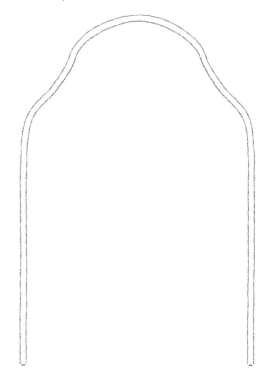

3 Insert the uprights through the holes in the bed base until the legs are 2.5cm long. Cut four strips of paper 2 x 2.5cm. Apply wood glue to these and roll them around the bed feet, with the 2.5cm dimension running vertically. The bed base thus rests on the thickened parts of the four feet.

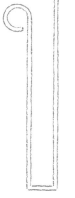

4 For the bed head, cut two 14.5cm lengths of 1mm wire. Shape as shown. Do the same for the other end of the cot.

5 Glue together as shown, by applying a drop of quick-setting wood glue at each point of contact.

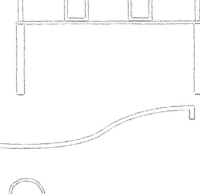

6 For each side, cut a 14cm length of 1.5mm wire and two 17.5cm lengths of the 1mm and bend to shape as shown.

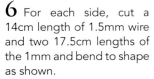

7 Glue in place as shown, using the quick-setting wood glue. Reinforce the joints with three or four turns of fine wire. Make the other side in the same way.

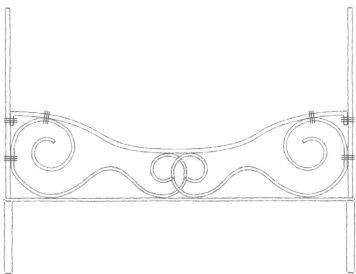

8 Cut a strip 0.2 x 27.5cm from thin Bristol board. Glue it all round the edge of the bed base to reinforce the holes where the bed legs pass through.

9 Coat the whole piece with gesso, leave to dry thoroughly, then paint off-white.

10 Cut a mattress, 6 x 11.5cm, from 10mm foamcore. Cover with cotton fabric. Attach a small caster to each foot.

You will need

- 1mm Bristol board
- Thin Bristol board
- Squared paper
- White florists' wire, 1mm and 1.5mm
- Gesso
- Satin-finish acrylic paints:
    black
    off-white
- Paintbrushes
- 000 wire wool
- Utility knife
- Flat-nosed pliers
- Side-cutting pliers
- Compass point
- Quick-setting wood glue
- Superglue (cyanoacrylate)

METAL WASHSTAND

1 Cut a tray 3.5 x 5cm and three edge pieces from 1mm Bristol board as shown. Score the back piece where indicated.

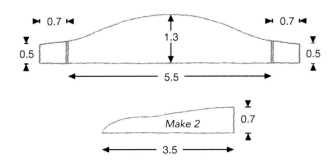

164

2 Cut the apron pieces to go below the tray from 1mm Bristol board. Score and bore small holes where shown.

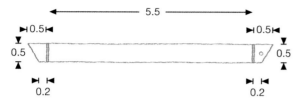

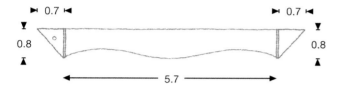

3 Cut the shelf, 3 x 5cm, from 1mm Bristol board. Cut notches 1mm square at each corner.

4 For the towel rail, cut a 4cm length of 1mm wire. Bend back 0.5cm at each end. For the legs, cut two 15.2cm lengths of 1.5mm wire. The idea is to make one front and one back leg together. Bend where indicated, then bend the end of the longer (front) leg outwards slightly, placing the pliers 2cm from the end.

5 Check that everything is square and parallel by laying the bent piece on squared paper, then adjust as necessary against the vertical lines on the paper. Recut one of the ends if need be so that both rest on the same horizontal line.

6 Bend the ends of the Bristol board pieces where you have scored them. Glue the back edge to the tray, and then the sides. Glue on the two apron pieces, then the legs, checking that the latter are precisely parallel.

Attach the shelf 2cm above the back feet (2.2cm above the front feet). Check from all sides that the shelf is parallel to the top.

7 Cut a strip of thin Bristol board, 0.2 x 18cm. Glue this all round the edge of the shelf and around the legs, to make the shelf more secure. Insert the towel rail into its holes with a drop of glue at each end.

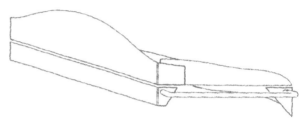

8 Coat the whole piece with gesso, then paint off-white.

If you want to simulate flaking enamel, once the gesso is dry, apply a coat of black paint. Leave to dry, then paint off-white. When dry, rub gently with 000 wire wool in the places you want to distress. Apply patina 1 (page 188).

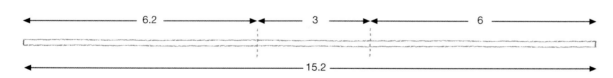

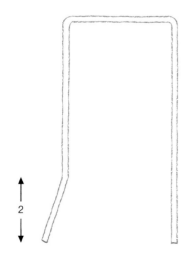

You will need

- 0.8, 1 and 3mm limewood sheet
- 1mm Bristol board
- Thin Bristol board
- Mirrored acetate
- 4 wooden banisters
- 4 hinges (8 x 10mm)
- 2 gold pins
- 12 gilt-paper flowers
- Satin-finish acrylic paint: off-white
- Paintbrushes
- Fine glasspaper
- Utility knife
- Clamps
- Quick-setting wood glue

DRESSING TABLE

1 From 3mm limewood sheet, cut a table top 3.5 x 8cm, two long apron pieces 1 x 6.6cm and two short aprons 1 x 2.3cm. Cut the top layer of the table top from 0.8mm lime, 3.2 x 7.5cm.

2 Glue the two layers of the table top together so that their back edges are flush and there is a margin at the front and sides. Clamp or weight until dry. Round over the edges with fine glasspaper.

3 Cut the legs from wooden banisters as shown and whittle them with the knife. Glue them to the short apron pieces. Glue the long aprons to these two assemblies, then fit the top.

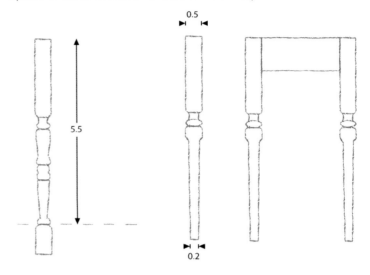

4 Cut the boxes for the drawers from 1mm lime. Cut the following pieces for each box and assemble as shown.

- Bottom (a): 1.4 x 1.8cm.
- Sides (b): 0.8 x 1.5cm.
- Back (c): 0.8 x 1.8cm.

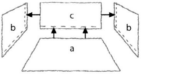

5 For the top of each box, cut one piece 1.7 x 2.4cm and another 1.5 x 2cm to glue on top. Soften the edges, then glue the top to the box, flush with the back edge.

6 For the mirror support, cut two shapes from 1mm Bristol board as shown and glue them together. Cut the notches and trace the curve by laying the mirror over it (see step 11). Glue the boxes to the table, keeping the back edges flush. Glue the piece of Bristol board between the boxes, again keeping the back edge flush. Adjust the notches as necessary to fit over the lids of the boxes.

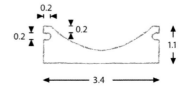

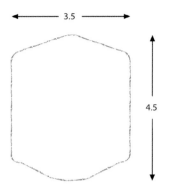

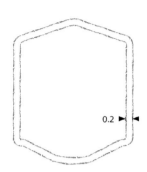

12 Do the same for the side mirrors.

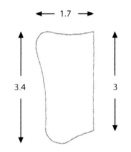

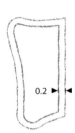

7 Glue on some paper flowers. Paint the whole piece off-white, avoiding the insides of the boxes so as not to impede the working of the drawers. Gently wipe off the paint on the flowers to reveal some patches of gold. For an aged effect, rub the edges with fine glasspaper, apply patina 1 (page 188) and wipe off until the desired effect is obtained.

8 For each drawer, cut the following pieces from 1mm Bristol board and assemble as shown.

- Bottom (a): 1.3 x 1.5cm.
- Sides (b): 0.6 x 1.4cm.
- Back (c): 0.6 x 1.5cm.

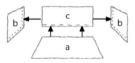

9 Cut the drawer front (d) from 1mm Bristol board, 0.7 x 2cm. Soften the edges. In the centre, trace a tiny cross with the tip of the utility knife. Cut the head end of a pin to 0.3cm for the drawer pull. Glue this to the centre of the cross. Glue d to the front edge of the drawer so the top of d is level with that of b.

10 Apply a coat of off-white to the whole drawer, inside and out. Wipe off the outside to reduce the build-up of paint while keeping the colour. Gently wipe the paint from the heads of the pins to reveal some touches of gold. Age and patinate as described in step 7.

11 For the central mirror, cut two identical shapes from 1mm Bristol board. Cut out the centre of one of them. Cut an identical shape from mirror acetate.

13 Give a coat of off-white to all the Bristol-board pieces, including the edges. Glue the mirrors to the solid pieces, then glue the cut-out pieces onto the mirrors with a sparing amount of wood glue. When dry, paint the edges of the three layers for a uniform effect.

14 Place the three mirror sections face down on a flat surface. Align them as indicated. Attach the hinges with superglue. Leave to dry flat, then glue the central part of the triptych to its support. Add a pleated ribbon made from a strip 8cm long (see the sofa, page 147, step 11).

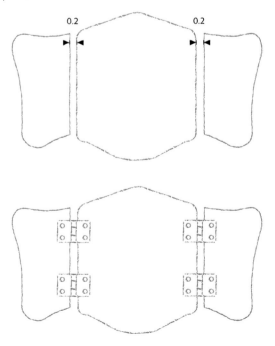

You will need

- 4mm sheathed electric cable
- Florists' wire, white, 1mm and 1.5mm
- 1mm Bristol board
- Thin Bristol board
- 10mm foamcore
- 10 gilt-paper rosettes
- Cotton fabric
- Gesso
- Satin-finish acrylic paint: off-white
- Paintbrushes
- Wire strippers or side-cutting pliers
- Scissors
- Utility knife
- Compass point
- Quick-setting wood glue
- Superglue (cyanoacrylate)

DOUBLE BED

1 Cut a bed base 12 x 16.5cm from 1mm Bristol board. Pierce a small hole at each corner, 1mm in, large enough to take the stripped ends of the electrical flex.

2 For the bed head, cut 32cm of electrical flex. Strip 2cm of flex at each end. Keep the ends of the sheathing and cut them to 1.8cm long. Shape the rest of the flex as shown.

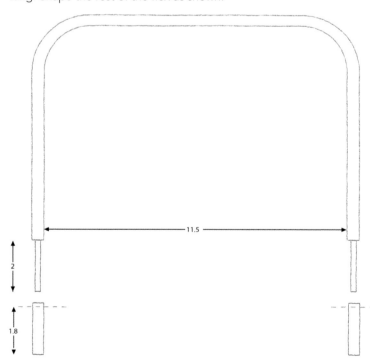

11.5

2

1.8

3 Cut two 11.5cm lengths of 1.5mm florists' wire. Dip each end in a drop of superglue. Glue to the base of the arched part as shown.

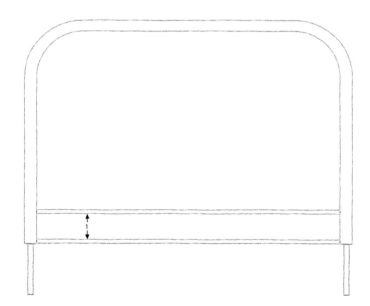

1

4 Cut 20.5cm of the 1.5mm wire and shape as shown. Dip each end in a drop of wood glue and glue to the upper crossbar of the bed head.

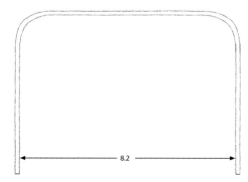

8.2

5 Cut two 1.4cm lengths of 1.5mm wire. Dip one end (in contact with the outer arch of electrical flex) in a drop of superglue, and the other end (in contact with the inner arch of florists' wire) in wood glue. Glue in place as shown.

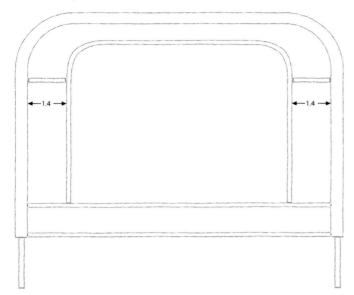

6 Cut five bars 6.2cm long from 1mm wire. Dip each end in wood glue. Glue inside the inner arch at intervals of 1.4cm. Glue paper rosettes at the top of each bar.

7 For the foot of the bed, cut 25cm of electrical flex and proceed as for the bed head.

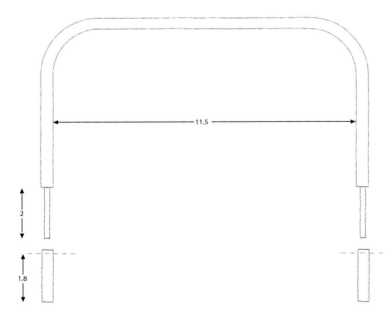

8 Cut an 11.5cm length of 1.5mm wire. Fix this 1cm from the base of the arch.

9 Cut 15cm of 1.5mm wire and shape as shown. Dip each end in a drop of wood glue and glue to the crossbar.

10 Continue as for the bed head, except that this time the bars are 3.4cm long.

11 Slip the feet through the holes in the bed base. Fix the bed base to the sheathing of the electrical flex with a drop of superglue. Slip the 1.8cm lengths of sheathing onto the bed feet so that the bed base is held between the two pieces of sheathing. Fasten with a drop of superglue. Use wood glue to stick a strip of thin Bristol board, 0.2 x 58cm, around the edges of the bed base to reinforce the leg joints.

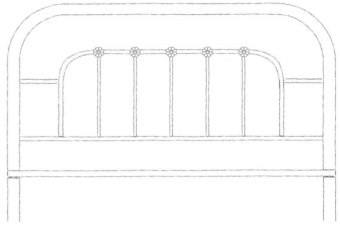

Completed bed foot

12 Coat with gesso, then paint gold.

13 Cut a mattress from 10mm foamcore, 11.5 x 15.8cm. To obtain the desired thickness, layer two or three pieces together and fasten with a few spots of glue. Cover with cotton fabric.

You will need

- 1, 3 and 10mm balsa
- Shell-shaped button or bead, approximately 1cm diameter
- Gesso
- Satin-finish acrylic paints:
    ivory
    raw sienna
    white
    black
- Gloss acrylic varnish
- Paintbrushes
- Fretsaw
- Utility knife
- Quick-setting wood glue
- Fine glasspaper

LOUIS XV CHIMNEYPIECE FOR THE ATTIC BEDROOM

1 Cut the outline of the fireplace and the two pillars from 10mm balsa as shown. Glue the pillars to the front of the chimneypiece, either side of the opening.

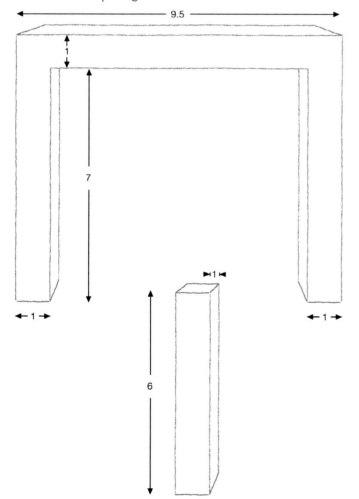

2 Cut the following shape from 10mm balsa with a fretsaw. Gently hollow the front in the places shown, using a round pencil wrapped with glasspaper.

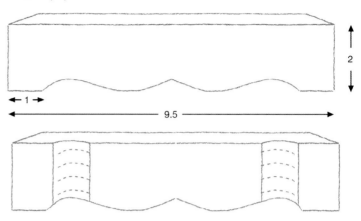

3 Place the shell-shaped button in the centre. Push down so as to leave an impression, then remove the button. Glue the block to the pillars and allow to dry.

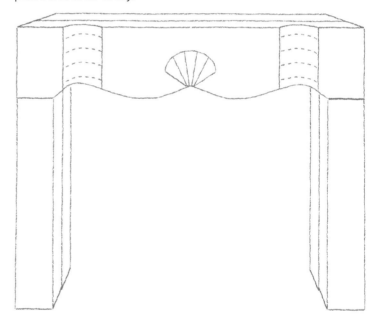

4 Round over all the front and side edges with fine glasspaper.

5 Cut the following shape with a fretsaw from 3mm balsa.

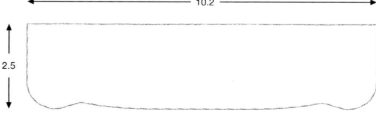

6 Fretsaw the following shape from 1mm balsa. Glue it on top of the larger piece as shown, and clamp or weight until dry.

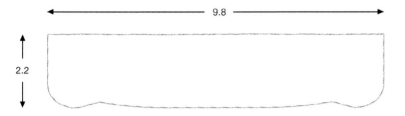

9.8

2.2

7 Round over the edges, except at the back, with fine glasspaper. Glue the mantelshelf to the chimneypiece.

8 Coat with gesso, then paint in imitation marble and varnish (see page 189).

You will need

- 1mm Bristol board
- Thin Bristol board
- Thin acetate
- Copier paper or thin cotton fabric
- Gesso
- Modelmaking paint, gold
- Paintbrushes
- Utility knife
- Scissors
- Masking tape
- Wood glue
- Solvent-free contact adhesive
- Clamps

SMALL FOLDING SCREEN

1 Cut two identical shapes from 1mm Bristol board. Cut openings in one of them as shown.

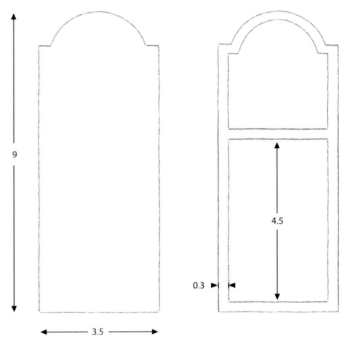

9

4.5

0.3

3.5

2 Cut one shape from thin acetate as shown.

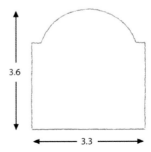

3.6

3.3

3 Cut four identical rectangles from 1mm Bristol board. Cut openings in two of them as shown. Cut two 2.8cm squares from thin acetate.

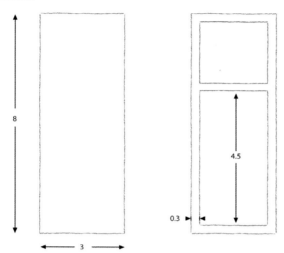

4 Apply a coat of gesso to all the shapes, including the edges. Paint the pieces gold all over.

5 Fix pieces of masking tape, creased along the centre, to the back of the screen with wood glue, as shown, being careful to keep all the pieces parallel (see page 152, step 3). Leave to dry.

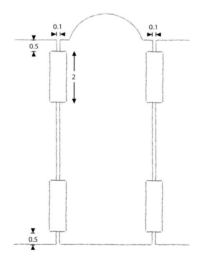

6 Print your chosen pictures onto paper. Lay the cut-out pieces of Bristol board over the whole pieces and mark where the openings come; then remove the cut-out pieces. Cut the printed paper pictures to fit the openings.

7 Cut three rectangles of printed fabric to cover the lower part of each section of the screen, leaving a gap of 1mm all round. Apply a thin coat of wood glue to the Bristol board, lay on the fabric and rub down firmly.

8 Lay the squares of acetate over the pictures; these 'windows' will be held in place between the two layers of Bristol board. (If necessary, add a drop of contact adhesive at each corner.) Glue the cut-out pieces to the whole pieces and weight until dry. Add a bow, as for the sofa (page 147, step 11).

You will need

- Round bulb with bulb holder and flex
- Thin Bristol board
- Florists' wire, thin
- Offcut of expanded polystyrene
- Light cotton or organza, white
- Cocktail stick
- White sewing thread or very fine wire
- Bead, 8mm diameter
- Sequin or jewellery finding, 9mm diameter
- 2 furniture casters, 2mm diameter (2 x 4mm including supporting bracket)
- Flat-headed metal pin
- Quick-setting wood glue
- Contact adhesive
- Gloss acrylic varnish
- Modelmaking paint: white lacquer
- Paintbrushes
- Pleating tool, small
- Compass point
- Side-cutting pliers

CEILING LIGHT FOR KITCHEN

1 Cut the lampshade from thin Bristol board. Cut along the radius and overlap the edges by about 1.5mm.

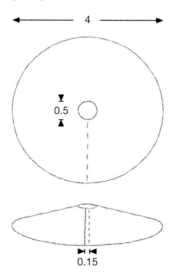

2 Cut a strip of fabric 2cm wide by about 20cm long. Pleat this strip with the pleating tool (see page 155, note and step 4).

3 Glue the pleated fabric to the shade as shown. Cut off any surplus in the length of the fabric. Smooth down the pleats onto the Bristol board to avoid excess thickness. The 0.5cm of extra width forms a scalloped border.

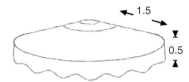

4 Varnish the whole of the lampshade, including the fabric border. The aim is to simulate cast glass (*pâte de verre*) by creating an effect of uneven translucence through the varnish overlying the Bristol board and the thin fabric. Leave to dry thoroughly before assembly.

5 For the counterweight, join the sequin to the bead with contact adhesive. Paint with white lacquer.

Tip

For ease of painting, spear the bead with a cocktail stick. Stick this into the polystyrene while the paint dries.

6 For the metal stay, cut 1.5cm of thin florists' wire. Form the rings by bending around a cocktail stick. The stay should not be longer than 0.9cm overall.

7 Place the top of the lampshade over the bulb holder (1). Pass the flex through one of the rings in the metal stay (2). Run the upper caster onto the flex (3). Fix the caster in place where the upper support will be, 6.5cm above the lampshade, by bending the flex around it (4). Pass the flex through the other ring in the stay (5). Slide on the second caster (6). To make the lower support, fix the caster 4cm below the first one by bending the flex around it (7).

8 Attach the counterweight to the second caster (8) with a piece of thread (or thin wire) inserted into the base of the bead. Bring this thread up through the counterweight and out at the top. Pass it through the supporting bracket of the caster. Put a spot of contact adhesive on the top of the counterweight. Bring the thread back through the counterweight, pulling it until the top of the sequin is flush with the base of the caster bracket. Cut the threads flush with the base of the bead.

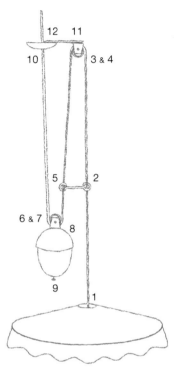

9 Push the head end of a pin, cut to 0.5mm long and dipped in contact adhesive, into the base of the counterweight (9); this should fix the thread inside the counterweight.

10 Thread on the sequin (10) with its flat surface uppermost (this side will later be glued to the ceiling). Cut a strip of Bristol board 0.2 x 1cm. Glue one end of this to the top of the supporting bracket of the first caster (11). Glue the other end inside the sequin (12). This maintains the correct distance between the caster and the sequin, the two components which will be glued to the ceiling.

You will need

- 1, 2, 3 and 5mm limewood sheet
- Quick-setting wood glue
- 3 x 10mm grooved moulding (architrave)
- Mirrored acetate
- Flexible Plexiglass
- 8 steel pins
- 4 brass doorknobs (buttons)
- 2 brass drawer pulls
- Brass lock escutcheon
- 000 steel wool
- Paintbrushes
- Woodstain: antique wood
- Fretsaw
- Side-cutting pliers
- Needle-nosed pliers
- Utility knife
- Clamps

KITCHEN DRESSER

Note

To avoid any marks caused by excess glue, all parts should be stained on both sides before assembly. The piece is assembled once the stain is completely dry. If you prefer to paint the dresser, this can be done after assembly.

UPPER SECTION

1 Cut the following pieces:

From 2mm limewood sheet:
- A (back): 9.5 x 7.5cm
- B and B' (sides): 3 x 6cm

From 1mm lime:
- C (top): 3 x 8.9cm
- D (base): 3 x 8.9cm

Frame members for sides, 1mm lime:
- a: 0.5 x 7.5cm (make 2)
- b: 0.5 x 5cm (make 2)
- c: 0.5 x 2cm (make 4)

2 Glue the frame members to the sides as shown, then assemble the upper cabinet; the dotted lines show the positions of the edges.

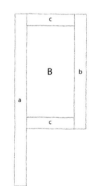
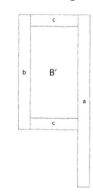

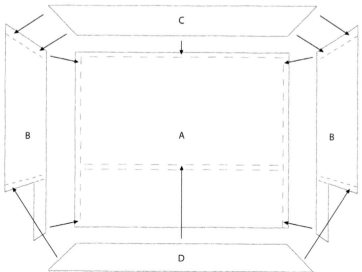

3 Cut a shelf (E) from 1mm lime, measuring 2.5 x 8.9cm. Glue halfway up the inside of the cabinet (2.5cm from the top).

4 Cut the finishing strips for the midsection of the dresser from 1mm lime (make two of each):

- d: 0.5 x 2.5cm
- e: 0.2 x 8.3cm
- f: 0.2 x 2.1cm

Cut a 2 x 4cm mirror and glue this between strips f as shown.

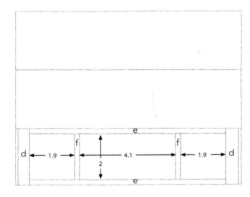

5 From the 3 x 10mm grooved moulding, cut two pieces 7.5cm long (g), two pieces 8.3cm long (g') and one piece 3.8cm long (g''). Cut the four pieces g and g' in half lengthways to make mouldings 0.6cm wide. On the back of the two pieces g', groove as indicated to accommodate the pivots for the doors.

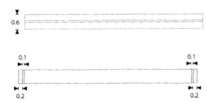

6 Glue on the mouldings as shown.

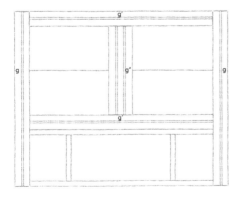

7 Cut two pieces (j) 0.4 x 8.3cm from 3mm lime to cover the grooves for the pivots. Glue them as shown.

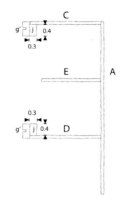

8 Cut a strip 0.5 x 2cm from 2mm lime. Glue this behind g'', right at the top. This piece acts as a doorstop, so the doors remain flush with the front of the cabinet and can't be pushed inside.

UPPER DOORS

1 For each door, cut the following pieces from 1mm lime:

- h: 0.5 x 3.7cm (make 4)
- i: 0.5 x 2.5cm (make 4)
- h': 0.3 x 3.4cm (make 2)
- i': 0.3 x 3.5cm (make 1)

Assemble the frames (parts h and i) as shown. Glue the battens h' and i' to the back of one of these frames. Halfway up one of the pieces h, make a hole for the doorknob. Start by marking a cross with the utility knife, starting across the grain. Slightly enlarge the centre of the cross with a compass point dipped into a drop of wood glue. Glue the other frame (h and i) to the battens. This creates a groove for the windows to be inserted into the doors.

Note

To simplify the hanging of the doors, the windows will be installed after the hinges. This allows you to reach through the frames and hold them in place with one hand while you attach the pivots or hinges with the other hand.

2 Cut the pointed ends of four pins to 1.2cm. Holding the doors in place as described above, use needle-nosed pliers to push these pins through the grooves made at step 5, and into the doors.

3 Using the fretsaw, cut two trim strips from 2mm lime. Cut the lower piece to fit between the uprights.

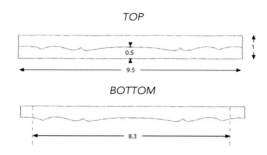

TOP

BOTTOM

LOWER SECTION

1 Cut the following pieces and assemble as shown.

From 2mm lime:
• A (back): 7 x 10cm
From 5mm lime:
• B (sides): 3.7 x 7cm (make 2)
• C (top): 4 x 9cm
• D (base): 3.7 x 9cm
• E (divider): 4 x 9cm

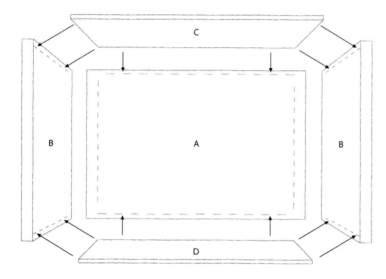

2 Cut a notch in piece E and make two small holes as indicated, using the point of a pin dipped in a drop of wood glue (these are for the door pivots). Glue this piece 1.1cm from the top of the lower cabinet of the dresser.

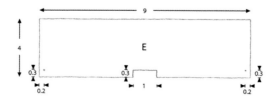

3 Cut the side frames and back legs from 1mm lime and assemble as shown.

• a: 0.5 x 8cm (make 4)
• b: 0.5 x 7cm (make 2)
• c: 0.5 x 2.7cm (make 4)

4 From the 3 x 10mm grooved moulding, cut two 8cm lengths (g), one 9cm (g') and one 6.5cm (g"). Cut the pieces g and g' lengthwise to create mouldings 0.6cm wide. On the back of g', cut grooves for the pivot pins as before (page 175, step 5). Attach these pieces as shown.

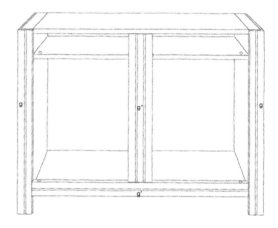

5 Cut a piece (j) 0.4 x 9cm from 3mm lime and glue to the base of the cabinet (D) to cover the grooves for the door pivots.

6 From 2mm lime, cut a strip 0.5 x 2.5cm to serve as a doorstop. Glue it to the underside of the divider E, behind g".

LOWER DOORS

1 For each door, cut out the parts listed below.

From 2mm lime:
• p: 3 x 5.2 cm
From 1mm lime:
• h: 0.5 x 5.2cm (make 2)
• i: 0.5 x 2.9cm (make 2)

2 Glue the parts from 1mm lime (h and i) to the solid door panel (part p). Make holes for the doorknobs as you did for the upper section.

3 For the top of the lower cabinet, cut a rectangle 4.5 x 1cm from 2mm lime and another 4.3 x 10.5cm from 1mm lime. Glue the smaller piece on top of the larger, leaving a margin all round except at the back, where the two pieces are flush. Clamp or weight until dry.

4 Round over the edges with fine glasspaper. Glue on the top and install the doors.

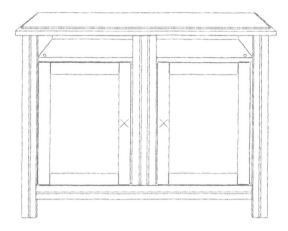

DRAWERS

1 Make two identical drawers from 1mm lime, assembled as shown.

- a (back): 1 x 3.9cm
- b (sides): 1 x 3.6cm (make 2)
- c (bottom): 3.6 x 3.7cm
- g (front): 3 x 10mm grooved moulding, 3.9cm long

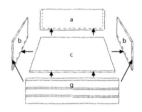

FINISHING TOUCHES

1 Assemble the upper and lower sections of the dresser. Glue a brass knob into the hole in each door, and a brass pull in the centre of each drawer. Insert the glass panes (2.9cm square) into the frames of the upper doors. For the 'cathedral glass' effect, see page 35 step 4.

You will need

- 1mm and 1.5mm limewood sheet
- Gesso
- Side-cutting pliers
- Pointed-nose pliers
- Utility knife
- Quick-setting wood glue
- Superglue (cyanoacrylate)
- Thick metal foil
- Flexible acetate
- Offcut of expanded polystyrene
- Modelmaking paints:
    white lacquer
    metallic silver
- Satin-finish acrylic paint: black
- 1mm florists' wire
- 8 dressmaking pins
- Canson paper, black
- 5 brass doorknobs (buttons)
- 4 gas burners
- Wire oven shelf

COOKER

1 Cut the control panel (piece F), 1 x 4.5cm, from 1.5mm limewood.

2 Stick the five brass buttons into an oddment of polystyrene for ease of handling, and lacquer them white. Paint six dressmaking pins in the same way. Pierce a hole in piece F at each of the places marked by a cross. Put aside (the knobs will be fitted at a later stage).

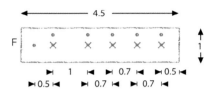

Note

To make a hole in a strip of wood without splintering, use the tip of a utility knife. Make a shallow incision, 1mm long, across the grain of the wood, then another at right angles to the first. Where the two cuts meet, insert a compass point that has been dipped in a drop of wood glue. Press gently to enlarge the hole.

3 For the oven door, cut the following pieces from 1.5mm lime and assemble as shown.

- a, a': 0.6 x 4.5cm
- b, b': 0.5 x 3.5cm

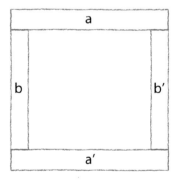

4 Cut a frame from the black Canson paper as shown (this will be glued to the back of the door). Cut the glass panel from acetate, 3.5 x 3.7cm.

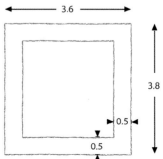

5 All the parts for the drawer are cut from 1mm lime, except piece a which is 1.5mm. Cut and assemble as shown; parts a, b, b' and d are glued around the edges of part c. The bottom edge of the drawer front is flush with the base; it does not project at the bottom.

- a (front): 1.5 x 4.5cm
- b, b' (sides): 1.2 x 4.4cm
- c (bottom): 3.8 x 4.5cm
- d (back): 1.2 x 4cm

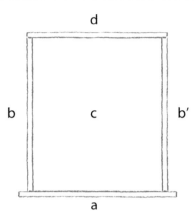

6 Cut the following pieces from 1mm lime to form the lid of the cooker. Assemble as shown, gluing the smaller pieces around the edges of piece c.

- a: 0.2 x 0.5cm (make 2)
- b: 0.2 x 1.5cm
- c (lid): 4.3 x 4.9cm
- d, d': 0.2 x 5cm
- f: 0.2 x 4.5cm

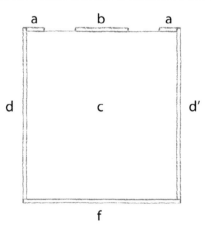

7 For the body of the cooker, cut the following parts from 1.5mm lime and assemble as shown. The dotted lines show where the edge of one piece is glued to the inside face of another. Clamp until dry.

- A (back): 4.2 x 6.85cm
- B, B' (sides): 5 x 7cm
- C (base): 4.2 x 4.8cm
- D (top): 4.2 x 4.8cm

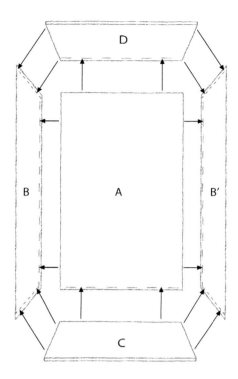

13 Make the drawer handle in the same way, using 2cm of wire.

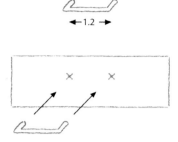

14 To finish the lid, cut two strips of metal foil 0.4 x 1cm for each hinge, and cut two 0.9cm lengths of dressmaking pin. Proceed as described on page 36. To attach the hinges, one leaf is glued flat to the top of the cooker lid, and the other is glued to the back of the cooker (piece A).

8 Apply a coat of gesso inside and out. Paint the inside black. When dry, paint the outside with white lacquer; two coats may be needed to give an enamel-like finish. Paint the other parts of the cooker similarly.

9 For the gas rings, cut four 1.5cm circles from the black Canson paper. Fix them symmetrically to the hob with wood glue. Glue the metal burners on top using superglue.

10 Glue the painted buttons and pins to piece F.

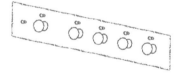

11 Place the acetate between the wooden oven door and the internal panel of black paper. Glue the paper to the inside of the door using only a sliver of glue along each edge; the acetate does not need gluing because it is sandwiched between the wood and the paper.

12 For the door handle, cut a 4.5cm length of wire. Bend back 0.4cm at each end, using the pliers. Make a hole at each of the positions marked with a cross. Dip the ends of the handle in a drop of superglue and glue in position.

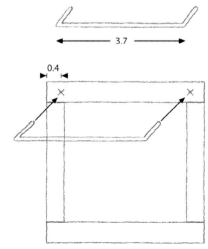

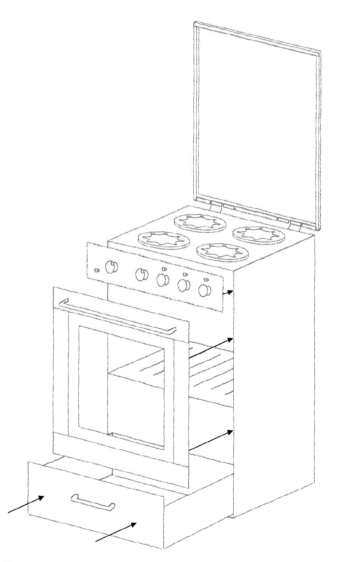

15 Slide the drawer into position, glue the wire shelf into the oven, glue on the door and then the control panel.

You will need

- 2, 6 and 10mm balsa
- Utility knife
- Quick-setting wood glue
- Compass point
- 2 clamps
- 1 nail, 5mm diameter
- Filler
- Fine glasspaper

KITCHEN SINK

1 Cut the base (A) from 2mm balsa, 2.5 x 6.8cm. Make a hole with the compass point, then enlarge it with the nail.

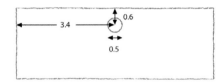

2 Cut the following pieces.

From 6mm balsa:
- C (back): 1.5 x 8cm
- B, B' (sides): 1 x 2.5cm

From 10mm balsa:
- D (front): 1 x 8cm
- E, E' (supporting walls): 3.5 x 5cm

3 Assemble as shown, using wood glue. Clamp until dry.

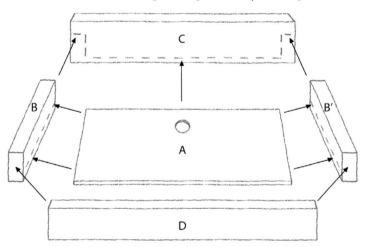

4 Glue the supporting walls E and E' beneath the sink.

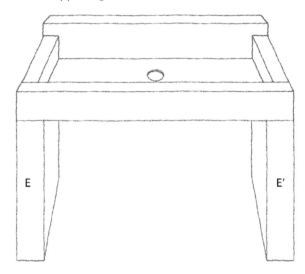

Note

The supporting walls are 0.6cm narrower than the sink. When the sink is installed, the remaining space leaves room for pipework underneath. Alternatively, the supports can be made to run the full width of the sink.

5 Gently round over the edges with fine glasspaper. Coat the whole structure with gesso. When dry, cover with filler (being careful not to build up too much thickness) to give a stone effect. Leave to dry before smoothing the surfaces with fine glasspaper if necessary. Leave as it is for a white stone sink, or paint whichever shade of stone you prefer. Apply patina 1 (page 188). A wall-mounted tap and exposed pipe would be appropriate for this kind of sink.

METAL CHAIR

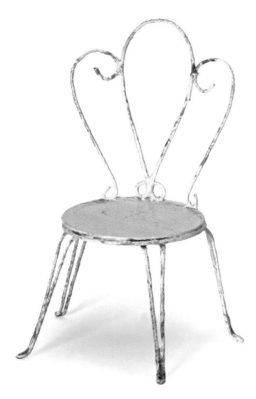

You will need

- 1mm Bristol board
- White florists' wire, 1mm
- Needle and white sewing thread
- Gesso
- Satin-finish acrylic paint: white
- Paintbrushes
- Scissors
- Side-cutting pliers
- Chain-nosed pliers
- Compass point
- Quick-setting wood glue
- Superglue (cyanoacrylate)

1 Cut the seat from 1mm Bristol board. Pierce four holes with a compass point, 1mm from the edge, as shown.

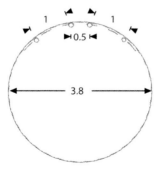

2 Cut a 12cm length of wire. Form into a circle, overlapping the ends by 0.5cm. Bind the ends together with sewing thread.

3 Glue the wire hoop to the underside of the Bristol board so that the joint in the wire falls between the middle two holes.

4 For the central part of the back, cut 13cm of wire and shape as shown, using chain-nosed pliers, which have flat, pointed ends.

5 For the side pieces, cut two 7cm wires and shape as shown.

6 Assemble the parts with wood glue. Reinforce the joints with sewing thread if necessary.

7 Place the back against the rear part of the seat so that each loop is aligned with one of the holes; to achieve this you will have to bend the sides forward a little to follow the curvature of the seat. Sew the loops to the seat as follows: cut about 40cm of thread, fold it in two, then insert this double thread into the needle. Pass the needle through one of the holes from the underside, then put it through the wire loop. Pass it back down through the same hole, then through the loop formed by the thread beneath the seat. Pass it through the remaining loops without breaking the thread. After sewing the last wire loop, tie off the thread with a double knot below the seat. Cut off the excess thread and place a drop of wood glue at each of the holes where the thread comes through.

8 For each leg of the chair, cut 9cm of wire. Fold in two, then shape as shown.

9 Superglue the legs to the underside of the seat at equal intervals.

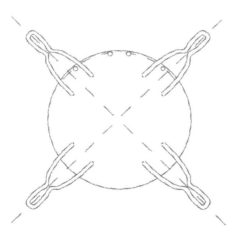

10 Check that all the components are accurately positioned. When the glue is completely dry, coat the whole piece with gesso then paint satin white.

Note

Since this chair is made of metal, water-based acrylic paint may cause natural rust patches. If you prefer your chair to look pristine, use an oil-based paint or a rust-resistant lacquer instead.

PEONIES

STEMS

1 Cut one stem per flower from very fine wire, about 4cm long. Smooth out a strip of green crêpe paper about 0.4mm wide and apply glue to about the first 1cm of it. Wrap this around the end of the stem. Wind it around until the whole stem is covered, holding the paper firmly between thumb and forefinger throughout.

2 Cut off the excess paper. Dip the end in a drop of glue. Continue to hold it firmly for a while between thumb and forefinger, spreading the excess glue along the length of the stem. Make as many stems as you intend to make flowers.

Colouring

1 Cut a strip of white crêpe paper, 2.5 x 20cm. Smooth it out, which will increase its length to about 27cm.

2 Paint one side of this strip, mixing red and white watercolours with plenty of water to give different subtle shades of pink. Along the edge, add a little more red as desired for the heart of the flower, or add a touch of dilute blue to give a faded effect. Any shade from white to burgundy is suitable for peonies.

3 Lay the painted strip flat on a perfectly smooth surface and leave to dry completely. The paper may shrink a little as it dries, so smooth it out again if necessary.

Small petals (A)

1 Fold the strip of crêpe paper in two across its width. Fold in two again, and then a third time.

2 Trim the edges of the folded paper with scissors. Cut the small petals for the heart of the flower by notching the paper as shown. Cut them 0.4cm long. This results in 64 small petals.

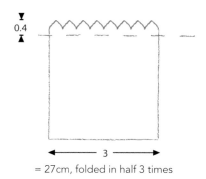

= 27cm, folded in half 3 times

3 Lay the strip of petals flat on the offcut of foamcore, having first removed the paper film from one side of the foamcore to produce a foam work surface.

4 Cut off the point of a cocktail stick and round the end slightly with fine glasspaper. Use this tool to emboss each of the small petals, all along the notched edge of the paper strip.

Large petals (B)

From the same folded strip of paper, cut the large petals as shown. Cut them 0.5cm long.

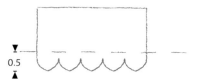

Petals (C)

1 From what is left of the folded strip, cut a half-petal shape along the fold. The number of folds allows you to make several different sizes with one snip of the scissors (0.5 x 0.5cm for the largest petals; those formed from the inside of the folded strip will be smaller). Cut about 16 petals in this way.

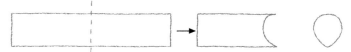

2 Emboss each petal with the tip of a pastel crayon, white or pink depending on the shade required.

Heart of the flower (D)

1 From what is left of the paper, cut a strip about 0.3cm wide.

2 Dip one end of the stem in wood glue. Twist the strip of crêpe paper around the end so as to obtain a round heart about 0.4cm in diameter.

3 Cut off the excess paper and spread glue uniformly over the heart, rubbing it well into the paper. As you do this, you can shape the heart with your fingers into a neat sphere.

Sepals (E)

1 Cut a 6cm square of dark green crêpe paper. Smooth it out; this will enlarge it to about 6 x 8cm. Fold as you did for the petals (A).

2 Cut a half-sepal shape (E') across the fold of the paper as shown.

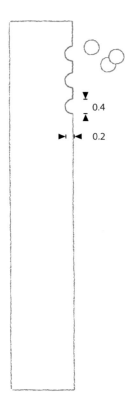

ASSEMBLING THE FLOWER

1 Apply glue to the whole of the underside of the heart (D). Glue the first petals (A) to the base of the heart, against the stem.

2 Wrap the strip of petals (B) all around the heart (D + A). Add a spot of glue after every three or four turns, as the strip is wound around the heart.

3 Pinch the base of the flower to shape the calyx. Use the whole strip of petals to make a full-blown flower; use fewer petals for a smaller flower.

4 Using tweezers, place a few petals (C) around the heart (D + A + B); dip their bases in a drop of glue, then place them around the base of the flower, preserving the convex shape.

5 Emboss three of the sepals (E') and use the tweezers to place them around the stem at the base of the flower, having first applied a smear of glue.

BUDS

Form a small heart (D), then glue three lightly embossed sepals (E') around it.

LEAVES

1 Fold a strip of green crêpe paper as for the petals (A), and cut out the leaves (F, F').

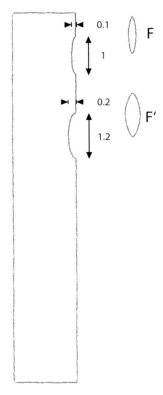

2 Apply glue to the whole length of a piece of dark green sewing thread. Leave it to dry, by which time it will be somewhat stiff. Cut 3cm of this thread.

3 Glue about 1.2cm at one end and attach the first leaf (F'). With tweezers, dip the extreme ends of the other two leaves (F) in a drop of glue and place them on either side of the first leaf.

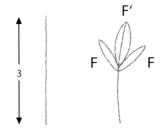

4 Glue the leaves and stem to the stem of a flower or a bud.

Hydrangeas

You will need

- The same tools and materials as for the peonies, plus a little lichen
- Colours: white, blue, yellow and pink

Assembling the flower head

1 Dip the end of the stem in wood glue. Roll and press a small piece of lichen around the glued end of the stem. Form a head no larger than about 1cm diameter.

2 Using tweezers, pick up the individual flowers by one of the petals. Dip the back of each flower into a drop of glue, and place it onto the lichen. You will need 20 to 30 individual flowers for each stem. To represent the branching of the flower head, leave some lichen visible in contact with the stem.

Stems and colouring

1 Make the stems as for the peonies.

2 Colour a 5 x 20cm strip of white crêpe paper as for the peonies. Use a mixture of white and red. Add a touch of dilute blue or a mixture of blue and yellow to give a faded effect.

Flower heads

1 The flower heads of hydrangeas consist of multiple branchings, each of which carries an individual flower. Fold your coloured band of crêpe paper as for the peonies and cut out the individual flowers.

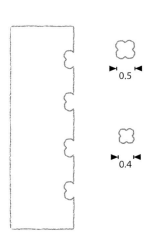

Leaves

1 Make the leaves from green crêpe paper, using the same method as for the peony leaves.

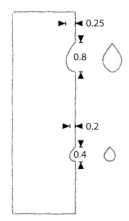

2 Cut and stiffen the thread as for the peonies.

3 Glue a large leaf to the end and bend the stem back at a right angle. Glue a second large leaf opposite the first.

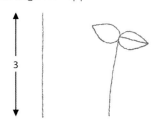

4 Glue two more large leaves opposite one another, 0.5cm away and on an axis at 90° to the first pair. Glue two small leaves 1.5cm from the second pair and parallel to the first pair. Make at least one stem of leaves per flower head.

5 Arrange the flowers into a round bouquet in a vase, flowerpot or garden urn.

Tip

It's easier to cut with the scissors if you grip the folded strip of paper between thumb and forefinger and turn it as you cut, so that the paper moves rather than the scissors.

2 Lay each flower on your piece of foamcore with the top layer removed (as for the peonies). Press the centre of each flower with the rounded end of a cocktail stick (as for peonies).

ROSES

STEMS AND COLOURING

1 Make the stems as for the peonies.

2 Stain two 5 x 20cm strips of white crêpe paper as for the peonies. Use a mixture of white, yellow and red, then stain the second strip in a more intense shade of the same colours.

PETALS

1 Fold the lighter of the two strips, cut out the petals and shape them by embossing on the foamcore pad as you did for the peonies.

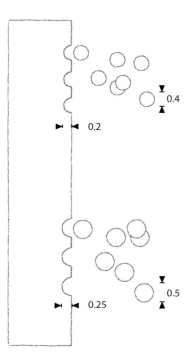

ASSEMBLING THE FLOWERS

1 Form the heart of the flower from the darker strip, using the same method as for the peonies; make some round and some oval heads.

2 Cut a strip 3mm wide from the darker strip of paper. Wrap this narrow strip around the heart (as for the peonies), taking care at the base of the flower that the paper does not wind around the stem. Use the whole of this narrow strip for a full-blown flower, and less of it for a more closed flower.

3 Using tweezers, arrange some petals around the heart; begin with the smallest, dipping the base of each petal into a drop of glue. Use the tweezers to shape one or two of the petals by bending their tips outwards.

4 To make buds, glue three or four small petals around a small heart.

LEAVES

1 Make the leaves from green crêpe paper, using the same method as for the peony leaves.

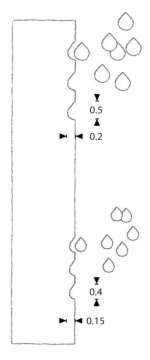

2 Cut and stiffen the thread as before.

3 Apply glue to about 0.5cm of the end of the thread and attach a first leaf. With the tweezers, place two more leaves, one either side of the first, having dipped the base of each one in a drop of glue. Add two more leaves below. You can place as many as seven leaves on each stem, in which case, use the small ones.

3

4 Glue the stem of leaves to the stem of a flower or bud.

PAINTS AND PAINT EFFECTS

FILLER

For a flaking effect, dab the filler with a sponge before it dries.

For a trowelled effect, make circular movements when the filler is beginning to dry.

For a stone effect, smooth out the filler evenly before it starts to dry.

PATINA 1

Mix equal parts of burnt umber and raw sienna, with the addition of odour-free white spirit. By way of example, for 30cl of white spirit you will need 1cm of burnt umber and 1cm of raw sienna (measured as it comes out of the tube).

PATINA 2

Mix three parts burnt umber and one part raw sienna with white spirit. For 30cl of white spirit, measure 3cm of burnt umber and 1cm of raw sienna.

Note

You can vary the patina effect by combining these two recipes: more raw sienna for a faded look, more burnt umber for a stained effect. In this way, for example, you can darken the foundations of the house or particular parts of the furniture to simulate long-term wear.

BRICKS AND EARTHENWARE

1 Apply a coat of gesso and allow to dry. Mix equal parts of English rose and chestnut brown. Apply a coat of this mixture and allow to dry.

2 Mix ivory and caramel in the same proportions. Apply a coat of this mixture and wipe off while still wet so as to expose the first coat of paint in places. Leave to dry.

SLATE ROOFING

1 Coat with gesso, leave to dry, then apply a coat of mid-grey acrylic paint. Allow to dry.

2 Mix a dark grey from one part black to two parts silver. Mix this grey with the mid-grey in equal parts. Apply one coat of this mixture.

3 Wipe off this coat with 000 steel wool while still wet; this will give the colour more subtlety.

4 Apply patina 1 and wipe off gently with 000 steel wool, then do the same with patina 2, avoiding those parts of the roof that are covered with zinc.

IMITATION ZINC PAPER

1 Choose aluminium packaging paper (sold by stationers); this comes in rolls 70cm to 1m wide and is more robust than cooking foil. Cut a strip 20 x 70cm across the width of the roll.

2 Paint it all over with silver modelmaking paint. For ease of handling, leave this to dry; being solvent-based, this paint dries more slowly than water-based acrylic. However, if you proceed to use the paper before it is completely dry, the zinc effect will be all the more realistic: finger marks and other imperfections will give it a pitted appearance, as though worn away by the weather. The aluminium colour of the foil will be revealed in places through the paint. Gentle abrasion with 000 steel wool can accentuate the metallic effect of the zinc.

Note

Another method is to gesso a sheet of thin Bristol board. Allow to dry completely, then finish with a coat of silver modelmaking paint. This method gives the appearance of brand-new zinc.

RED FLOOR TILES

1 Apply gesso all over and leave to dry.

2 Apply a mixture of cream and caramel in equal parts. While still wet, dab on little spots of burgundy. Blur the transitions between colours. Apply smudged touches of chestnut brown. Leave to dry.

3 Dab on touches of caramel and wipe off.

PINK MARBLE (FOR SALON CHIMNEYPIECE)

1 Apply a coat of gesso to the whole structure.

2 Paint English rose; while still wet, add touches of tan, dabbing with your finger to blend the tones together.

3 Repeat the operation with light grey. Put this colour on with a lighter touch. Before all this is dry, add the white veins of the marble.

MARBLING

1 There are several methods of imitating marble; the degree of realism depends on the fineness and softness of the veining. A sliver of paper, barely half a millimetre wide, cut from the edge of a piece of thin Bristol board, will do the trick. You will have to replace it once you have used it a few times, because the paint will soften it.

2 Dip this strip of paper into the paint, then gently wipe off the surplus. Drag it across the areas you want to cover, finishing with a slight zigzag movement so as to blend naturally with the previous colours, which are still wet.

3 Allow to dry thoroughly. Apply gloss varnish, then again leave to dry thoroughly.

LIGHT MARBLE (CHIMNEYPIECE FOR ATTIC BEDROOM)

1 Apply a coat of gesso to the whole of the structure.

2 Paint ivory, then apply touches of raw sienna while still wet, dabbing with your finger to blend the tones together.

3 Repeat the operation with light grey. This colour is applied with a lighter touch. While still wet, add black veins.

MAIN COLOURS FOR THE HOUSE

The names of colours are often identical from one manufacturer to another, but the shades themselves may vary (as with fabric dyes). In the colour scheme used for this house, ivory is close to straw yellow, off-white is the colour of vanilla, and cream is actually off-white. It's best to choose your colours from a manufacturer's colour card to get the best match with the colours used here.

Roof

Landing walls (to dado height)

Façade

Kitchen walls (to dado height)

Front door

Salon panelling

Window catches

Landing and hall walls

Nursery

HOUSE GALLERY

Houses evoke strong feelings, however simple they may be – houses that have lived give off an atmosphere of majestic serenity. Not all of my creations are portrayed in this book, since some of them are no longer in my possession, but here are the stories of all of them…

TOWN HOUSE
(DECEMBER 1990–JANUARY 1991)

For this first house, my parents got the plywood cut to size for me, based on a quick sketch on paper. It measures 80cm wide by 40 deep and 120 high. This house boasts nine main rooms, plus a ground-floor entrance hall and a first-floor landing. To begin with I made only the basic structure, unsure exactly what kind of façade to give it. I was much more interested in the interior decor. The house is now awaiting restoration…

A CHARMING RESIDENCE
(DECEMBER 1998–JULY 1999)

This house of 19 rooms was conceived and created between 1998 and 1999. Measuring 90cm wide, 50 deep and 125 high, the house is constantly evolving; the entrance hall, bathroom and studio are still awaiting finishing touches.

This house gave rise to all the subsequent ones. It was the first draft of the Château which would soon take shape. All the *petit-point* carpets, cushions and samplers which adorn my miniature rooms were first created for this house; this is where I carried out my first experiments with printed fabrics made on an ordinary printer. It bears the impress of all my sources of inspiration: rustic chic in the ground-floor salon, grand 18th-century country-house style in the big faded-pink salon on the first floor, Venetian palazzo style in the little boudoir adjoining the green bedroom on the second floor, Swedish style in the little Gustavian sitting-room, shabby-chic in the small blue-grey

salon of late 19th-century inspiration, Provençal country style in the bedroom hung with printed fabric… Above all, the pink bedroom brings together a range of themes which have been further developed in my later projects: folding screens, fans, fire screens, patchwork, draped double curtains, imitation *pâte de verre* and faux-marble chimneypieces.

This house was also fundamental to my method of designing houses, especially the concept of perspective, of rooms behind rooms that give extra realism to an interior. There is always another room to be glimpsed through a half-open door, just as in a real house.

Whenever possible, I have always arranged for the staircase – even though it is present from the ground floor to the attic – to take up as little space visually as possible. It's not unusual to see a whole room sacrificed – even more than one, depending on the number of floors – in order for the staircase to be fitted in in a logical manner. But I have made a point of reducing its visual impact in all my houses. The staircase is generally placed against the further wall, with an internal wall in front of it, its position depending on the available space and the need to fit in (or suggest) half-landings. A space is then left in front of the partition wall for an extra room. That's how I made room for the little Gustavian salon, the bathroom and the skylit studio.

A HOUSE IN THE COUNTRY
(18TH-CENTURY SWEDISH STYLE)
(OCTOBER 2001)

For this project I set myself the challenge of creating a house on the smallest possible budget. I used the cheapest wooden house kit available at the time, and furnished all the rooms with precut kit furniture which I customized myself. Made on a shoestring, this house was put together in three

weeks and is still awaiting its opening front wall. Whitewashed floors, aged wood panelling, worn gilding, dark pictures on the walls… everything epitomizes the Swedish style in this serene and restful house in the country.

THE FAMILY HOUSE
(JUNE–AUGUST 2003)

Romanticism is the theme of this house, with its eclectic assortment of furniture, accumulated over generations. A passion for flea markets is combined with a love of George Sand and her novels. The furniture mostly consists of revamped pieces in natural wood, give or take a few items created from scratch such as the washbasin-cupboard in the bathroom, the slab sink in the kitchen, the folding screen and cheval glass in the boudoir. All the items are painted or stained and waxed; some have been refurbished to give them a more typically French style.

THE CHALET (FEBRUARY 2004)

This is the smallest 1/12 scale house I have made so far: just 47 x 30 x 45cm. I made the whole structure from a kit. The decor is mostly based on textures of wood and stone, to recreate the cosy atmosphere of a little house tucked away in the mountains.

THE VETERINARY CLINIC
(APRIL–JUNE 2004)

The clinic is entirely homemade, except for the sanitary fittings, the bedroom light and some pans in the kitchen, as specified in the brief for this project. It forms part of the village of Miniaturama-sur-Mer, a collaborative project which brings together nearly 100 houses and around 30 miniature scenes: roadside stalls, a market place – everything that's needed to make a village truly alive and welcoming.

The vet's house has been fitted out as a clinic and consulting room for pets (you'll notice that this vet further specializes in feline ailments). It also features a little shop selling food and accessories for cats and dogs.

THE FLORIST'S HOUSE AND SHOP
(SEPTEMBER 2004–JULY 2005)

The design of the house and shop began in September 2004. Construction would begin in December 2004 and last until July 2005. I built it all myself, from the basic wooden structure to the furniture and accessories, except for one or two items such as the dining-room chairs and the living-room armchairs (repainted and re-covered with fabric printed on an office printer) as well as the sanitary wares and the writing desk in the little study. I gave a day-by-day account of the building of this house in my blog (atelier-de-lea.fr). It brings together all of my enthusiasms – antiques, flowers (especially roses), the timeless charm of eloquent old houses, cats (obviously), paintings, old china, lace… in short, the spirit of the countryside.

THE BASTIDE
(JULY–SEPTEMBER 2005)

In this Provençal farmhouse I have tried to recreate the characteristic atmosphere of that magnificent region. A region steeped in history, with a style that looks towards Italy – a return to the source of our civilization.

THE CHÂTEAU
(MAY 2004–PRESENT)

This project took hold of me in May 2004 when I discovered the book *La Vie de château* by Jean-Bernard Naudin and Christiane de Nicolay-Mazery (Editions du Chêne). On opening it, I was stunned by the sight of a bedroom as simple as it was sumptuous, bathed in sunlight. I just had to recreate this room in miniature! Since the only suitable setting for it was a stately home with huge rooms, only a château would do. Sadly, the dimensions of such an edifice as I imagined it were simply out of the question for the living room where I have set up my little studio corner. Not having the space to make the whole building in one piece, I therefore opted for a modular construction: each room is freestanding but they can be joined together quickly and, most conveniently, they can be stacked for storage. At last the adventure can begin!

THE HOUSE FROM THIS BOOK
(JULY 2006–JANUARY 2007)

This project was born one fine day in July 2006, when I received a message full of promise: a proposal for a book…

DENTELLES ET RIBAMBELLES

This model is a 1/12 scale copy of the shop which I founded with Pascal in 1993. After 22 years in the heart of Montmarte (Paris), you can find Dentelles et Ribambelles exclusively online (www.dentelles-et-ribambelles.fr/en/). The website specializes in miniatures, accessories, furniture, display cabinets… all in 1/12 scale. You'll also find my own handmade unique creations at La Boutique de Léa (https://www.etsy.com/shop/AtelierdeLea).

Dentelles et Ribambelles
www.dentelles-et-ribambelles.fr/en/

Originally published in France as *Le Grand Livre de la Maison Miniature*
© Fleurus Editions, Paris, October 2008

First published 2014 in English by
Guild of Master Craftsman Publications Ltd
Castle Place, 166 High Street, Lewes,
East Sussex BN7 1XU

Reprinted 2015

ISBN 978 1 86108 954 0

Publisher Jonathan Bailey
Production Manager Jim Bulley
Managing Editor Gerrie Purcell
Senior Project Editor Dominique Page
Translator and Editor Stephen Haynes
Managing Art Editor Gilda Pacitti

Set in Avenir
Colour origination by GMC Reprographics
Printed and bound in China

To order a book or request a full catalogue of GMC titles, please contact:

GMC Publications Ltd
Castle Place, 166 High Street,
Lewes, East Sussex,
BN7 1XU
United Kingdom

Tel: +44 (0)1273 488005
www.gmcbooks.com